GOING WITH GOD!!

PATH TO PEACE AND JOY!

— ♥ —

By Christine Craig Seckel

Going with God

Trilogy Christian Publishers

A Wholly Owned Subsidiary of Trinity Broadcasting Network

2442 Michelle Drive

Tustin, CA 92780

For information, address Trilogy Christian Publishing

Rights Department, 2442 Michelle Drive, Tustin, CA 92780.

Trilogy Christian Publishing/ TBN and colophon are trademarks of Trinity Broadcasting Network.

For information about special discounts for bulk purchases, please contact Trilogy Christian Publishing.

Manufactured in the United States of America

10 9 8 7 6 5 4 3 2 1

Library of Congress Cataloging-in-Publication Data is available.

ISBN: 978-1-68556-577-0

ISBN: 978-1-68556-578-7

TABLE OF CONTENTS

1. God as my Guide .... Page 7

2. Patterns of My Life .... Page 9

3. Heartbreaks .... Page 15

4. Baptism of the Holy Spirit .... Page 45

5. Presence of God! .... Page 49

6. Mighty Miracles! .... Page 53

7. Bounteous Blessings .... Page 65

8. My Special Angel! .... Page 79

9. Nine Paths to Happiness, Peace, and Joy! .... Page 107

10. Labor of Love .... Page 121

Dedication

——— ♥ ———

To my Loving Father God, our Blessed Mother Mary, my Lord and Savior Jesus Christ, and to my dearly beloved husband, Thomas Garaway Seckel.

Acknowledgements

——— ♥ ———

With thanksgiving to the Lord, my heartfelt gratitude goes out to my dear friends, Barbara Balut, Mary Bascone, and Chiaki Taylor, for all their encouragement, help, and support, as I embarked upon my most joyful job for God!!

I also extend my deepest appreciation to Trilogy Christian Publishing Company for their outstanding efforts to help make my God-given message available to all those who peruse these pages! Thank you all.

CHAPTER ONE

❤

God As My Guide

"Our God will be our guide for ever and ever."
Psalms 48:14 (KJV)

"Who made you?" God made me. "Why did God make you?" God made me to know Him, to love Him, and to serve Him. Those words are etched in my memory from my earliest days in Sunday School at St. Ambrose Catholic Church in Bridgeport, Connecticut. Little did I realize then, from ages seven or eight, how significant they would become to me – and the depth of meaning that would emanate from them -- over time.

And, even more than that, how these words would show me the depth of God's love for me. And how much He loves ALL of us. And blesses ALL who trust in Him and place their lives completely in His ever-loving protective hands.

This, of course, does not mean my life would be easy and there would not be trials and tribulations. But it did mean that, though there were hardships and heartbreaks, these would be overshadowed by God's mighty miracles, boundless blessings, and in-depth teachings -- which would eventually lead to a beautiful life filled with peace and joy!

As I opened my heart to know God and His great Love for me, I would receive deep revelations about the Baptism of the Holy Spirit and the meaning of perfect love casting out all fear – from our LIVING LORD Himself. I would learn, not only to pray, but to listen – to LISTEN and to HEAR – His Words of Wisdom that would guide me through each day. This would eventually lead me to understand how God was working and weaving the patterns of my life through all events – whether delightful or distressful – into His perfect whole!

He would take me from poverty to plenty; from one where I wondered if I could afford to go to college, to one of becoming highly educated; from one of desperate loneliness, to one of feeling fully loved, completely devoid of loneliness; and with gifts I didn't even know I needed. Yes, God did make ALL things work together for good!
(Romans 8:28)

And, I believe, our Lord will do the same for YOU and ALL who open their hearts to learn more about Him. Through some of my experiences, with God as my Guide, and with the nine paths to happiness, peace, and joy I've outlined in a later chapter, I pray your walk with our Heavenly Father will deepen and bring greater understanding of what it means to truly give your life to Him. And as this occurs, result in a greater sense of purpose, accomplishment, and satisfaction for you -- in a life filled with peace and joy!

CHAPTER TWO

♥

Patterns of my Life

"For the eyes of the Lord run to and fro
Throughout the whole earth, to show His might
In behalf of those whose heart is blameless toward Him."
2 Chronicles 16:09 (KJV)

Before I delve more deeply into God's revelations, please allow me to go back to my meager beginnings. This will hopefully help you to more easily understand how God wove the patterns of my life into His perfect whole.

I was born and baptized Margaret Elizabeth Mills (Margaret, after my mother, and Elizabeth after my mom's mother) in Bridgeport, Connecticut. My nickname to my family was "Honey" and to my classmates, I was Margie Mills. I would later become Christine Craig because I was a part-time actress and singer.

At age four, my younger sister, parents and I moved into a low-income housing project called "Success Park," which I guess now looking back, was prophetic. Life was quite difficult then because my father was a Friday-night alcoholic. He many times would spend much of his weekly paycheck from General Electric Company on drinks at the local tavern. My mother

EASTER SUNDAY

"Having fun at the park when I was age five!"

——— ♥ ———

would send me quite a few miles from home to spy on him to see if he was there, which did not put me in his good graces.

Spending cash on alcohol, left little money for food and other essentials, and we sometimes wondered whether we would have our next meal. My father was also sometimes physically and verbally abusive to me. Other times, he would threaten my sister and me that he would use his belt on us if he thought we had misbehaved. I think about that now and it still brings terror to my heart. It is so important for parents to understand the impact their behavior has on a small child. Though it's important to set guidelines and give loving guidance, the threat of corporal punishment or abuse of any kind from someone who is their child's whole world, can be devastating.

But getting back to my main story. To help with household income, my mother took in ironing so somehow or another we managed to get by. However, I did at times, have anemia because I wasn't getting enough iron in my diet. My mother, who was mostly loving at the time, was later able to find enough funds so I could take voice lessons and for my sister and me to study piano. I don't know how she did it, but she did!

I loved to sing and at age five I knew most of the popular songs I heard on the radio. I am grateful to my mom for all she sacrificed in those early years and especially for making sure I received piano and voice lessons, which were very helpful in later life. She encouraged me to sing because her mother had been a church soloist, and she had always wanted to be a singer, too. I think because this didn't happen, she probably wanted to fulfill her dreams through me.

Things started to improve financially when I was about ten years old. As a result of fervent prayer and a promise made to my Grandma Mills on her death bed, my dad stopped drinking "cold turkey." After that, he built a two-bedroom home for us almost completely by himself.

Before then, when I was nine years old, I started babysitting three small children for fifty cents an hour. It seems strange, but I actually did a better job caring for them than their mother who was a college graduate. After that, my mother was convinced that going to university was detrimental to becoming a good mother. Therefore, she was not thrilled when she learned I wanted to go to college to study journalism after high school.

When I was in eighth grade, I enrolled in the College Preparatory Curriculum in high school, but my mother told me she and my dad could not afford to send me to university. I was quite sad and disappointed that I would have to change my high school studies and not go to college.

At the time, I was actively going to church, and I even evangelized two of my girlfriends to become Catholic, as well. I also remember having a very close relationship with God. His loving guidance must have been with me as I wondered how to go to university without my parent's help. Then it came to me! I reasoned that, if I switched to the high school Secretarial Curriculum, I could work my way through college with my secretarial skills.

So, I continued babysitting and began my high school studies. When I was sixteen years old, because of my shorthand and typing abilities, I got a job as a secretary at an insurance company. I went to school in the morning, worked in the afternoon, and went roller skating most evenings.

A year before my high school graduation, my dad was transferred from Bridgeport to Utica, New York by General Electric, where he became head of a large department. This was amazing, since he had only finished eighth grade. He was, however, quite intelligent and sometimes would read an entire book in one night.

At the time, I didn't want to move from Bridgeport to Utica, partially because I loved roller skating. My skating dance partner and

I had come in first for Connecticut and third for New England at a recent competition, and I wanted to pursue skating. I had a choice because my skating partner's parents told me I could live with them if I chose to do so.

My mom didn't want me to stay in Bridgeport, so she told me if I moved to Utica, I could go to college. So, I moved to Utica! Once there, however, my mother reneged on her promise. My dad, realizing this was wrong, told me SECRETLY he would help with some expenses if I wanted to attend Syracuse University. He had to be careful because if he did something that didn't meet with my mom's approval, she would become angry and not speak to him for two weeks. She treated me that way, too. One time, after my sister was married, she didn't speak to my sister's husband for a year because she said he insulted her. It wasn't until I talked to her about Christianity and forgiveness that she again began communicating with him. As it was, I never did need my dad's help with my college education. Someone else, with higher credentials, was looking out for me on that!

At this time, I was attending a Catholic Church in New Hartford, New York where our home was located. I was also singing in their choir. During the day, I worked as a receptionist at Utica College of Syracuse University. I was also taking two night classes at the college. One was an English course, which I attended on Friday evenings. As an extra-curricular activity, I was also helping in the Theater Arts Department with the play, *Harvey*. All parts for the play had been cast before I started, so I took a job as a set girl – I swept floors, did other errands, and helped cue lines for the actors, except the leading role of Myrtle Mae Simmons.

One Friday night, I was listening attentively to my English professor's lesson, when a knock came at the classroom door. The teacher was asked if I could be excused because there was an emergency, and my help was needed. This was opening night of *Harvey*, and the girl playing Myrtle Mae Simmons had had an appendix attack and was rushed to the hospital. The play's director asked if I could learn her lines (which were many) and go on stage the next night. I said I would try.

I stayed up all night learning almost all the lines and went on stage on Saturday evening. The people in the audience knew what had happened, so after the production was over, I was given a standing ovation and the director presented me with a bouquet of flowers. The story was also in the local newspapers, where one of the headlines read, "Set girl on Friday becomes Star on Saturday."

Shortly thereafter, the dean of Utica College called me into his office and kindly offered me a scholarship, so I could attend the university full time. I was, of course, flabbergasted and thrilled, and immediately accepted his offer! After that, I enrolled as a Public Relations major, which included many journalism classes.

Looking back, I imagine the scholarship was offered because of my participation in the play, but I also see now it was all part of God's plan. I understand, too, that He had answered my prayers in a most spectacular way! My Lord never ceases to amaze me! And He would amaze me even more in the years to come.

Other than my Catholic infant baptism and my dad's ability to overcome alcoholism, the university scholarship was God's first major blessing in my life! Little did I know there would be many more! And far greater than this!

CHAPTER THREE

———— ♥ ————

Heartbreaks

"The Lord heals the brokenhearted and binds up their wounds."
Psalms 147:03

This chapter is, by far, the most difficult for me to write. But, because it's important for you to understand how God can turn the most devastating life experiences into ones of blessings, I must plow through it. I know all of us have heartaches in our lives, and some are far worse than mine. But I would like to share a few of the significant ones that shaped the patterns of my life and led me closer to God. Through these events, He healed, taught, and molded me toward an abundant life of peace and joy, far beyond my greatest expectations. And it is all because I eventually depended upon and looked to Him for EVERTHING! We worked together and we were a team!

———— ♥ ————

The first and one of the most heartbreaking experiences I've felt was when my sister cast me out of her life when we were adults. My sister was two and a half years younger than I and, when we were growing up, my mother would often leave her in my care when she went grocery shopping. I was just six or seven years old when I began watching her, but I took the responsibility very seriously. My sister and my mother were everything to me in those days and I was completely devoted to them.

As the years went by, my sister and I were both married, and we each had two children. I loved her with all my heart and considered her to be my best friend. I was completely loyal to her, never ever saying or doing anything negative to or about her and I thought she treated me the same way. But now as I look back, I guess that wasn't the case.

When I was in my forties, I learned someone close to my sister had betrayed her trust numerous times. Though this was shocking to me, I didn't tell her what I knew because I felt it would hurt her deeply.

A few years later, she and I were having an in-depth conversation about the problems in her life, and I intimated I had further knowledge regarding her situation because I wanted to confirm what she was telling me. But I still didn't reveal what I knew. After that, it affected our relationship adversely. She became cool and distant, as she pulled away from our friendship. This, of course, was deeply distressing and depressing to me. From then on, she continued to hound me about what I knew. So, one day I abruptly blurted out the truth to her. Big mistake!

Instead of zeroing in on the person who harmed her, she became angry with me. It was a perfect example of "kill the messenger." Not only did this affect my relationship with my sister but she said things to my mother, who was also angry and would not speak to me. This incident caused estrangement, not only from them, but everyone on that side of the family. At the time, I was living in Florida, so I wasn't there to defend myself, though I doubt it would have made a difference.

Because it isn't pertinent to my message, I won't dwell on other aspects of this story. But what I will share is the deep betrayal I felt. Through this, an important part of my family was ripped away from me and the heartbreak was devastating! The irony is that I was the one who brought people together whenever there was a dispute amongst family members, and yet I was now the outcast.

Though this was heart wrenching to me, it did give me insight as to what Jesus must feel when He reaches out to mankind, and He is rejected. So, at least it was a learning experience to empathize with the Lord I love so much! It also helped me understand the feelings of others who have undergone similar circumstances.

That was the end of my relationship with my mother and sister, though my father and I communicated until he left this life to be with our Lord at age 91. I now speak with him in Heaven! And that's because of a significant change that took place in his life during his later years.

Though it was difficult to know my dad's heart, through most of his life he didn't show much evidence of a relationship with God, if any. He attended the Catholic church off and on, but when he went it seemed to be out of obligation to my mother, rather than something he wanted to do.

It wasn't until I was visiting him when he was older, and he asked to go to church with me, that I noticed his heart softening toward the Lord. There was also evidence of this another time when a Catholic priest was visiting our home and my dad proudly told him I always studied my Bible. This surprised me. I noticed then that perhaps he was beginning to realize the importance of God's Presence in one's life.

It wasn't until a few years later though, when he was recovering from a heart attack at age 82, that a significant life-changing event occurred

"Enjoying time with my eighty-year-old dad, Bill Mills!"

—— ❤ ——

for him! At that time, my father prayed with the same Catholic priest, and his relationship with the Lord took on new meaning. Something happened during that prayer that brought my dad closer to God. And this seemed to impact his life immeasurably! *"Thank you, Lord!"*

I praise God for my father's conversion because I can now relate to him spiritually in Heaven. Otherwise, that wouldn't occur! What happened too, is that once he went to be with Jesus, I was immediately closer to my dad than ever before. Our hearts became one in the Spirit, and it felt so good to have that kind of relationship with him. Right now, as I write about him in these pages, I strongly feel his presence with me. *"Thank you, Jesus, for that!"*

With respect to my mother and sister, what happened in our lives was very sad indeed – though I do have forgiveness in my heart toward them. My mom has since passed away, and I pray she is in Heaven with Jesus. My sister has had opportunities to contact me but has never done so. And though I have trust issues with her, I did reach out once by sending her photos and signing the accompanying note, "Love, Honey," but she never responded.

Though I have insight into some of my mom's and sister's motivations now that I am a psychotherapist, it's often difficult to fully understand people's hearts and why they act as they do. I realize too that sometimes God removes others from our lives for our own good. I accept that. And so, I leave it to Him!

The second heartbreak I experienced came with my first marriage. My husband was a highly intelligent Jewish boy from Brooklyn, New York, with an IQ of about 150. He was Dr. Chumley in the play, *Harvey*, which was mentioned in chapter two, and that's how we met. He was lots of fun and smart, and I loved him with all my heart.

After two years of dating and both of us attending Utica College, we went to New York City for the summer. I was living and working in Manhattan as a secretary, and he was working and living at home with his parents in Brooklyn. I was also taking voice lessons and attending St. Patrick's Cathedral church services. In September, he was planning to go back to Utica College, and I had just been accepted at Columbia University. I was going to remain in New York and continue working there while going to school.

Instead, we impulsively at the last minute, decided to get married so we could be together. Shortly thereafter, we were wed at the Unitarian Church chapel on Lexington Avenue in Manhattan. We then moved back to Utica where I worked in the public relations department of Mohawk Airlines, and he worked at the WRUN radio station as a disc jockey. He also attended college and subsequently received his Bachelor of Arts degree in public relations.

After that, my husband worked as a reporter for the Syracuse Post Standard newspaper in their Oneida bureau, so we moved to that tiny town not too far from Utica. Several months later, I gave birth to a baby girl, and I was at home caring for her.

This was a very desperate and lonely time for me because my husband was gone most of the day and worked evenings until ten. He also had our only automobile. There is an explanation for part of this, which will be clearer as I explain my story.

I also at this time had no real closeness with my mom because she didn't like my husband, though she did help for a few days with the baby. It would be several years before I had no relationship at all with my mother, but at this time I really needed her, and I longed for the love that only a mom can give. I really missed her. But she was angry with my husband, therefore that meant she was also angry with me. So, I was alone with an infant much of the time and very, very sad and lonely.

After working in Oneida for a year, my husband was offered a job as a reporter for the Wall Street Journal in their Philadelphia office. So, we moved to southern New Jersey, across the river from the City of Brotherly Love. We had a lovely elderly woman who cared for our three-month-old daughter, so I was able to start working again.

I got a job at the Philadelphia Carpenter's Union on Spring Garden Street testing apprentices, who wanted to become carpenters. I also put out a monthly newspaper for the union. I did all the writing, editing, headlines, captions, and graphics, until it was ready for the printer. I really loved that job! It satisfied all my desires to be a writer and other creative abilities.

But after a year, I had to leave my job because of the sexual advances from my boss. He was becoming bolder in his attempts and would literally chase me around my desk, trying to kiss me! He of course was not successful, but I was getting tired of dealing with it. So, I quit. They didn't have sexual harassment laws in those days. And the powers-that-be probably wouldn't have cared or believed me if I said anything.

While in southern New Jersey, I decided to continue my studies to complete my bachelor's degree in communications. I applied to Rutgers University in Camden, but I was told I needed more high school credits to do so. So, after two years of college, I went back to high school. I took algebra, geometry, and two years of Spanish. Then, I was accepted at Rutgers where I took college algebra, psychology, and English literature classes. I was glad I had gone back to high school because a little more studying never hurt anyone. I also really loved learning!

By this time, our daughter was over four years old, and I had just given birth to another girl. It was then, four years after starting his job with the Wall Street Journal, that my husband was transferred from Philly to the Journal's Los Angeles bureau. So, the four of us moved to southern California, where we eventually bought a home in Malibu.

Because my husband was Jewish and I was having doubts about my Christian faith, he and I decided when we wed to attend the Unitarian Church. This religion had only two tenets: 1. Belief in one God, and 2. Belief in the brotherhood of man. Beyond that, we were to study other theologies and philosophies and come to our own conclusions about our faith.

This did not work well for me because, during my marriage and attending the Unitarian Church, I always felt a void in my life. I knew something was missing, but I had no idea what it was. It was puzzling because God had answered all my childhood prayers: To go to college, to be married, and to have a daughter with curly hair. YES, curly hair! Can you believe I would pray for something like that? (And of course, my daughter hated her curly hair, which she later had straightened.) Though all my prayers were answered, instead of feeling complete inside, I felt completely empty!

After a few years, my husband quit his job with the Wall Street Journal and opened his own documentary film business. I was at home caring for our two daughters and investigating whether to pursue a singing career.

At the time, I was a soloist with the Unitarian Church Choir in Santa Monica and was accepted, after auditioning, to study at the Los Angeles Music Center, which was a huge honor. But it was quite a distance from home, and I had to care for my two children. So, after much serious thought, I decided to decline the offer. However, I did continue to sing and investigate opportunities that might be available for a pops' singing career. During this time, after ten years of marriage, I learned my husband had been unfaithful to me many times throughout our married life.

Professional photo, as I embarked upon a singing career!

Thus, the reason I was alone so much and so lonely after our first child was born. And some of the reason for the emptiness I felt. Because of this, I left him for two weeks. He begged me to return, and I said I would come back if he'd end the unfaithfulness. I also told him I wanted him to put me and the children first in his life -- which had previously NOT been the case. He promised he would. I went back and our lives together were better, though a lot of the emptiness I felt inside still lingered. I would one day realize the cause for that. But not yet!

The loyalty lasted for about six months and then the infidelity began again. With that, I filed for a separation. I received the Malibu home in the resulting divorce, and my husband received the documentary film business, which were of equal value.

My husband would later brag to my older daughter that he had been unfaithful to me far more often than I knew. I was shocked he would admit something like that to his own daughter. But this made me realize even more he was never the right choice for me in the first place.

Still, it was heartbreaking to realize I was part of a failed marriage. But I also knew life must go on, and I must make the best of it. Hopefully, it would be a learning experience. And, though it may seem strange, it was not difficult for me to forgive my husband. I guess I knew we all have our weaknesses, and we are all a work in progress. Now I pray for him and his salvation almost every day.

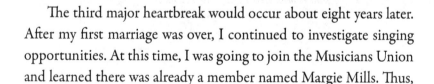

The third major heartbreak would occur about eight years later. After my first marriage was over, I continued to investigate singing opportunities. At this time, I was going to join the Musicians Union and learned there was already a member named Margie Mills. Thus, the reason for my name change. As a result, I eventually changed my professional name to Christine Craig.

During this time, I got a job singing at a Malibu restaurant and nightclub for several months, until the owner was murdered. Speculation was that the Mafia had killed him, but it remained a mystery. As you might imagine, it was shocking and sad for all who knew him, especially his beautiful young wife.

While singing at the nightclub, I began dating a man who was not only good to me, but to my children. He was kind and loving and I really enjoyed being with him. It was this man's influence that brought me back to Christianity when he invited me to attend a Malibu Presbyterian Church service with him. The pastor, Walter Gerber, was an outstanding Bible teacher, who was a Princeton Theological Seminary graduate. His sermons were educational, edifying, and inspiring!

It was uplifting for me to hear from someone like Walt Gerber because, before my first marriage, I had begun to have doubts about my Christian faith. This was partly due to a Utica College philosophy class textbook, where a Bible verse was taken out of context. As a result, I began to wonder if Jesus were truly God's Son. For twelve years, during my first marriage, I prayed asking God whether Jesus was His Son. But it wasn't until this time in Malibu that I began to get some definitive answers.

Wanting to investigate further, I continued attending worship services and Bible study classes at the Malibu church. To increase my knowledge, I read through the Bible twice. I wanted to grasp the entire message that threads through the Scriptures about God's plan for salvation, which would enable us to spend eternity with Him. (Incidentally, the paraphrased Living Bible is an excellent source for

Thrilled to be singing at a Malibu, California restaurant and nightclub!

anyone wanting to easily read through the Scriptures quickly. I use my King James Revised Standard Version in my daily devotions because I love the beauty of its poetic prose. And the Life Application Bible is good if you want to understand Bible verses and apply them to everyday modern life. I would also recommend Dr. David Jeremiah's Study Bible.)

In numerous ways, as I increased my biblical knowledge, God began to lift the veil from my eyes so I could eventually see that, YES, Jesus was truly our Messiah. That's when I again accepted Jesus into my heart as my Lord and Savior, as I had done as a small child. It was at this time that I began to think of Jesus, not only as God's Son, but also as my friend – someone with whom I could share my deepest thoughts and innermost feelings. I now had a personal relationship with Jesus Christ! And I was beginning to love my Savior more and more! It was then that I would again walk in a God-blessed and God-guided life! But it wouldn't be until a few years later that I would be shown by our Living Lord Himself that – definitively, beyond a shadow of a doubt -- Jesus was truly His beloved Son! There is more about this astonishing revelation in a later chapter.

As I became a stronger believer and Jesus was now in charge of my heart, my faith began to blossom! Now that I had a personal relationship with the Lord, it suddenly occurred to me one day that the emptiness I'd experienced for twelve years had completely disappeared! I was again WHOLE – I was complete in Jesus! And it felt so good to be fully ME again!

Not that those previous years were wasted! REMEMBER: "God, makes ALL things work together for good for those who love Him and are called according to His purpose." (Romans 8:28) It was in those years that I studied many different religions, theologies, and philosophies, so that I had a better understanding of my beliefs and the beliefs of others. This helped a great deal when I talked with friends about God and helped me better relate to them as I shared my testimony. I learned then that God wastes NOTHING!

It was during this time that I became active in the Malibu Presbyterian Church women's Bible study group. Shortly after I joined, the members voted for me to be their president. I really didn't understand "why" because they had been studying the Scriptures much longer than I had. So, I figured nobody else wanted the job! This turned into something quite positive though because it forced me to pray and speak in front of others. I had not before been comfortable doing this and it would later become invaluable to me. Again, part of God's plan!

These things all occurred while I was dating my new beau and now fiancé. After two years, we were married at the Malibu Presbyterian Church in a ceremony which included my two daughters, who were then ages seven and eleven.

Our lives were very full at that time. My husband and I were both active at the Malibu church, and I continued to sing as a soloist in their choir and at other Christian and civic events. My husband was a very active Malibu community leader, along with doing his job as manager of a local enterprise. I helped him with this by doing bookkeeping for his business. To expand my knowledge in that field, I also took general and tax accounting classes at Santa Monica College and UCLA.

After this, I enrolled part-time at Pepperdine University in Malibu to obtain my Bachelor of Arts degree in communications, which I had not yet completed. I took two classes – one in voice lessons and the other in theater arts. And to my amazement, I was offered a scholarship -- AGAIN WITHOUT ASKING -- by the theater arts department to attend Pepperdine full time. The only

'Lion in Winter' premieres

Appearing as Eleanor in "The Lion in Winter."

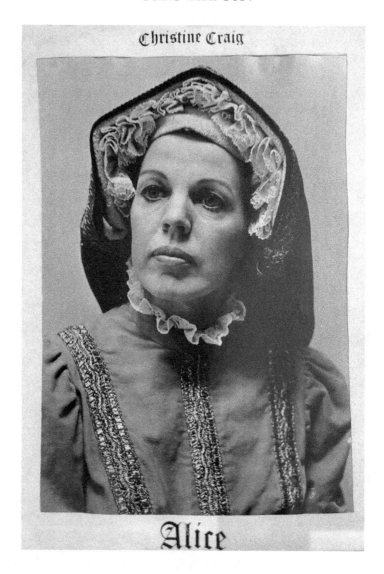

Acting in the role of Alice in "A Man for All Seasons."

requirement was that I appear in their performances each term, which was fine with me. This led to the lead roles as Eleanor in *The Lion in Winter* and Alice in *A Man for All Seasons*, along with roles in other productions. The scholarship was not only a major blessing to help me earn my bachelor's degree, but it eventually led to the female lead in eight Christian films, some of which were distributed around the world. I also became a member of the Screen Actors Guild.

However, underlying all the good that was going on in my life, there were problems -- as is often the case in most lives. No existence on Earth is perfect. And life with the Lord does not free us from difficulties, but peace within difficulties -- IF WE TRUST HIM to help us.

Within the first year of our marriage, I realized my husband had a serious problem with alcoholism. He would drink and drive and this terrified me because when he did, he would often cross over the center line on Pacific Coast Highway. There were many nights too when my older daughter and I would be looking for him along the road when he was late coming home, and we didn't know where he was.

All this was nerve-wracking, and the stress was making me physically ill. I also became concerned he could kill someone someday, and we could be sued and lose our Malibu home -- which was mine when we married. These days, he was seldom at home. And, when he was, he was not communicating with me. I imagine part of the reason was that I was very unhappy about his drinking, which caused me to be irritable and not very kind to him.

After six years of dealing with the alcoholism, I decided to get a legal separation to protect our home against a lawsuit. I hoped during the separation, my husband would get help and we'd eventually go back together because I still loved him. In California, the legal separation would become a divorce after a year, if either party signed the document and chose to make the divorce final.

Though it wasn't what I wanted to occur, this is exactly what happened! Because my husband wanted to date a woman who would not go out with him unless he was divorced, he signed the divorce papers. That liaison did not work out, but he would later marry someone who also drank too much. Years later, his alcoholism nearly killed him, and through his family's intervention, he finally stopped drinking. Now that I look back, I'm so glad I didn't have to experience all that.

But at the time, all this was devastating to me! I had lost the husband I so dearly loved and my relationship with my daughters was severely strained because they were both taking drugs with their boyfriends, who would later become their husbands. My life in Malibu, during this period, was sometimes very lonely and painful! And my only refuge was with our Heavenly Father and His Son, Jesus. There were many times when I would cry out, "Well, Lord, it's just you and me again!" Little did I know then that God would turn all these painful times into learning experiences and bounteous blessings.

Still, all these things did not stop me from serving God! I continued speaking and singing at different Christian functions. I was now leading the singles group at Bel Aire Presbyterian Church in Los Angeles, where I was also a soloist and sang in their church choir. Along with this, I enjoyed hosting many Bible studies and potluck dinners in my home with my new friends from the Bel Aire Church.

It was at this time that something interesting occurred! The Bel Aire singles group was quite large and consisted of mostly thirty- and forty-year-olds, with probably as many guys as gals. I knew some of the men were quite promiscuous and would go from female to female making their conquests. One day the Lord spoke to me and told me I needed to address this situation with the group. I, of course, said, "Okay," since it's not a good idea to say, "No," to God. But I also added, "I'll do it, but I'll probably never have another date." By this time, I felt so close to the Lord that it didn't surprise me to hear His voice through His Holy Spirit. You will learn more about this in later chapters!

At the next Bel Aire Singles meeting, I went to the podium, and started out by explaining that I had been getting a suntan in my front yard when the Lord spoke to me about something important. I also prefaced what I was about to say with, "As I speak about this, I will probably never ever have another date, but God has told me to do this. So, that's what I'm going to do." I then talked about the promiscuity that was occurring and that our Heavenly Father was not pleased. I continued by talking about Christianity, chastity, and the single life for about twenty minutes with words the Lord gave me. When I finished, I was now even surer nobody would ever date me again, which was alright with me because I knew I had no choice – I had to be obedient to God!

After that, the group and I formed a large circle and joined hands. I led them in song as we sang our Heavenly Father's praises. We always did this when we met, ending with our hands raised in worship to the Lord. These are the words we sang:

"I love you Lord and I lift my voice to worship you.
O, my soul, rejoice!
Take joy, my King, in what you hear.
Let it be a sweet, sweet sound in your ear.

"Offering praise, the sacrifice of my lips.
Offering worship, my hands extended to thee.
(We raised our hands to the Lord)

I love you, Lord. I love you, Lord. I praise and adore you, Lord.
I love you, Lord. I love you, Lord.
I give you all praise!
"Be exalted, O God, above the heavens!
And let thy glory be over all the earth!
Be Exalted, O God, above the heavens!
And let thy glory, let thy glory
Be exalted o'er the earth!"
(Psalms 57:5)

After the meeting was over, we all left and went home. I had no idea what the group thought about what I said.

Then, the most astounding thing occurred! After that, ten men called to ask if I would go out with them. I thought maybe they were testing me to see if I practiced what I preached. But, as I dated each one, they were perfect gentlemen, honoring what I said at the podium that day. I guess it does pay to be obedient to God!

During this time, I also concentrated on other aspects of my life. To support myself, I worked for a tax accountant for about a year. Then I opened my own general and tax accounting business in Malibu, serving some awesome clients -- many in the entertainment industry. I also rented part of my Malibu home to law students from Pepperdine University to supplement my income. Life was good again! And God was deeply ensconced in it!

— ❤ —

The fourth heartbreaking experience was with respect to my daughters. They were everything to me, and I would have done anything to protect them. Through their younger years, we enjoyed many activities together. Every night I helped them

Enjoying fun time with my pet calico cat, Tigerlily!

♥

with their homework, and we always had a sit-down session when we talked about our day and our feelings. We cooked together, played tennis and golf, and took ballet lessons. They were able to share anything with me without being judged, and they often shared intimate details about their lives.

I tried very hard to give them both equal attention to guard against jealousy, but when my younger child was in second grade, the teacher told me she was jealous of her older sister. We also had difficulties with her in those years because she had a problem with honesty.

But worse than that, in their late teens both girls began taking drugs. This had an adverse effect on them, and they became disrespectful and abusive toward me. Though I tried off and on for many years to relate to them, the abuse continued. Even though this occurred, I was still trying to set a good Christian example and be there for them, though they were not there for me.

One day, after sending a loving note to my older daughter, she responded by accusing me of something false and told me to "never e-mail her again." And I haven't heard from her since. I imagine the untrue information came from her sister who still had a problem with jealousy and honesty. She had done this before and the older one, without checking with me, seemed to accept what she said, even though the older one knew her sister had a problem with truthfulness. This was later somewhat confirmed because, though I e-mailed my younger child after that, she never responded, and I never heard from her again either.

After this happened, I was DONE. There comes a time, after you've been hurt and beaten down so many times, when you become numb. This was THAT time! I was done dealing with the drama and being treated so disrespectfully. I finally had to gladly give them back to God because He knows better than I how to deal with them. There is far more to this story and my daughters' issues, but I've chosen not to dwell on it. Again, I felt completely betrayed. And my heart was broken as I lost the children I so dearly loved. But who have chosen not to share those same feelings for me.

You may ask why God would allow these heartbreaks to occur, but He gives each of us free will to choose Him and His Love -- or to choose the devil's tools, some of which are drugs, alcohol, jealousy, and dishonesty. That's what free will is all about! God wants us to love and obey Him because we WANT TO, not because we HAVE TO -- He does not want us to grudgingly accept His will, but to lovingly want it because we love Him, and we know He loves us.

Accepting His will brings with it true happiness, peace, and joy! But it is up to us to choose to walk with Him and treat others with loving kindness in an abundant satisfying life -- or to travel in the devil's den of self-destruction and disrespect for others. My dad is a perfect example of someone who cast aside evil's tools and turned his life from one of failure into one of success -- and finally walking fully with God!

—— ❤ ——

A fifth heartbreak would come many years later. I was single and living in Florida when I met an intelligent fun-loving Jewish man who became a dear friend. We'll call him Dan, for privacy purposes. He was fifteen years younger than I, so I told him we could not date. Instead, he shared many stories about the different women he was seeing. He also fixed me up with one of his male Catholic friends, Bernie, who was closer to my age.

I considered Bernie a friend only, since I was not interested in having a serious relationship with anyone at the time. There also was no attraction on my part for him. Several months later, I was glad I had no strong feelings for him because this protected me from another heartbreaking experience.

Dan called me to let me know that Bernie had been attacked in the parking lot of a local shopping center. A drug addict tried to rob him, and Bernie made the mistake of fighting back. Six days later Bernie died in the hospital from his injuries.

The police caught the culprit who assaulted Bernie because he lost his sandal when he ran off after the attack. It contained the thief's DNA and, because he had a prison record, his DNA information was readily available. So, back to prison he went.

I often pray for and say "Hello" to Bernie, who hopefully is in Heaven now that he's gone. Though he was a Catholic and attended church every Sunday, he didn't seem to have much of a personal relationship with Jesus, if any. He had religion, but no relationship. There seemed to be no recognizable spiritual consciousness -- which is sad. I could be wrong about Bernie, but I saw no significant comprehension of what it meant to live his life with the Lord when I prayed with him before a meal or when I spoke to him about my spiritual experiences with God.

People miss out on so much when they lack spiritual awareness and fail to embrace the Lord's loving Presence in a close relationship with Him here on Earth. Life is also very limited when we fail to recognize and embrace God's vast spiritual world of love beyond our narrow and limited earthly existence! I pray what I discussed with Bernie influenced him somewhat and made his passing easier. And I hope and pray he is now enjoying life with our Loving Lord in Heaven!

Dan and I were of course shocked by what happened to Bernie, and we had many conversations about it and other life experiences. We often discussed our faith and, when we did, I tried to convince him his Messiah had come over two thousand years ago. I told him he didn't have to give up Judaism because Christianity included the Jewish faith. I also said Christianity was an extension of Judaism, so he need not feel he's being disloyal to his Jewish heritage, should he accept Jesus Christ as his Messiah and Savior.

I even explained using part of the wager by philosopher, Blaise Pascal, that God exists. I said, "If you gain by believing Jesus is the Son of God, and His death is an atonement for our sins, and it is only through Him that we can have a relationship with God, you gain all. If you lose, you lose nothing." I told him, all he need do is open his heart and ask God the Father to show him whether Jesus were truly His Son, just as I had done so many years before that. But all this fell on deaf ears.

Even when Dan was confronting a major crisis in his life, he was still trying to do things on his own. At the time I was prayerfully concerned about him. It was then that Jesus spoke to me and said, "Tell him to ask me, and I will help him." I told him what Jesus revealed to me and to this my friend responded with disdain and left. His life after that would become very difficult.

I was heartbroken he made the choice he made because his life was miserable after that, and I cared very much about his welfare. Dan and I are still good friends, and his life is better now. Still, I continue to care about his spiritual well-being, and I pray almost every day for his salvation. I also pray for and say "Hello" to Dan's mom and dad, who are now with God and now know their Messiah has come. I hope one day Dan will see this, too, and seek to live with Christ's sustaining Power and Presence!

———— ♥ ————

The last heartbreak took place after my second marriage was over. At that time, I went to Europe with a tour group to study the life of Martin Luther. After we visited many cities pertinent to Luther's life, one of our last destinations was the Wittenberg, Germany church where he was supposed to have hung his ninety-five theses on the door -- though this has been disputed by some historians.

Afterward, on the way back to our tour bus, I was walking along with some group members and enthusiastically talking to two German citizens. Without alerting me, the tour group turned off the road to another street that led to the bus parking lot. Unaware I was supposed to do this, I proceeded on until I realized the group was gone. I couldn't believe the tour members didn't alert me they were leaving the main road. Understandably alarmed when I could see no sign of them, I asked the Germans what I should do. They suggested I wait at a place where they said the tour buses passed by. And they left!

There I was standing alone in the middle of nowhere in a foreign land! I, of course, with great fear and trepidation, began praying vehemently for Jesus's help. Almost in tears, I said, "Please help me, Lord." Instantaneously, my bus appeared. *"Whew! What a relief! That was really scary!"* Thank you, Jesus! I waved at the bus and the driver stopped to pick me up.

But then the most awful thing happened! The tour leader, who was a Lutheran pastor, came bursting through the bus door and was furious because I had not gotten on the bus in the parking lot. He was ranting and raving! And he went on and on without giving me a chance to explain. Instead, he humiliated me in front of EVERYONE. I was stunned that he treated me so badly. And even if I could have said something, I was so shocked by his behavior I probably would not have had the words to respond. Later, I was in tears as I talked to my roommate, Priscilla, about it. She suggested I keep a low profile, which was not really the best suggestion. But that's what I did. Fortunately, this happened at the end of our visit to Europe.

(Incidentally, at the time I was too meek and uninformed to confront the tour leader and discuss the matter with him, so I said NOTHING! Today, I would have handled the situation much differently. Instead of crying and complaining to my roommate, I would have later calmly but assertively spoken to the pastor about it. I would have explained the facts about the incident and addressed the disrespectful way he treated me and his uncontrolled aggressive behavior, which certainly was no way for a Christian minister or anyone to act.)

Besides the problem with the pastor, I was puzzled as to why the group did not alert me they were turning off the main road. I had the feeling some did not like me, and the only reason I could think of was that I was a kind of free spirit, opting occasionally to prayerfully walk the streets of, say, Bergen, Norway, to talk to the townspeople and say "God bless you" to all I met -- rather than ride on a tour bus. I really felt led by the Lord to do this, and it also felt good to walk in the fresh air -- instead of sitting on a bus where I usually felt queasy from the gas fumes.

Doing this was the only reason I could think of why some members might dislike me, since I didn't know them that well. I was quite sure, though, they were judging me without knowing me. I also had no idea what they said to the pastor about why I hadn't gotten on the bus in the parking lot. This could explain why the minister was so upset, but still is no excuse for his behavior.

In the end, God would have the last word -- as He always does! It was an "all things work together for good" incident, as well as a teaching experience for ALL involved. On the evening before leaving Europe, some in the tour group put on a show for the other members. I was supposed to sing a solo and was the last to perform, which was no coincidence. Again, God's plan known only to Him! Before my song, I announced to the group, "THIS IS A PRAYER."

Then I proceeded to sing acapella, the following words:

Lord, make me an instrument of thy peace.
Where there is hatred let me sow Love,
Where there is injury, pardon,
Where there is doubt, faith,
Where there is despair, hope,
Where there is darkness, light,
Where there is sadness, joy!

O Divine Master, grant that I may not so much seek
To be consoled, as to console,
To be understood, as to understand,
To be loved, as to love.

For it is in giving that we receive.
It is in pardoning that we are pardoned,
And it is in dying that we are born to eternal life.

When I finished, the room was filled with a stunned, solemn

S
 I
  L
   E
    N
     C
      E

*"INFINITE LOVE for Mutter! ("Mutter" means "Mother" in German.)
On another European trip, I lived in Heidelberg, Germany for just a short
time with Mutter, but the love I felt, and still feel for her today, is BEYOND
MEASURE! This kind of Love comes only from up above!!"*

Chapter Four

Baptism of the Holy Spirit

"Blessed are the pure in heart,
For they shall see God."
Matthew 5:8

Probably the most significant event in my life was when I received the Baptism of the Holy Spirit! I was thirty-four years old and married to my second husband when it happened.

It had been an extremely difficult first year of our marriage because my husband's mother was dying of cancer. I called her Mother Pearl. And, though I knew her for only three years, we had a very strong bond – so special that after she died, she left me her copper wedding ring which I treasure to this day. I loved her with all my heart and the stress of her impending death caused me to become physically ill with colitis.

When Mother Pearl was in the hospital and had only days to live, my friend, Shirley Arends, and I visited her. The three of us prayed together and two days later Mother Pearl went to be with Jesus. During the prayer, I strongly felt the Presence of God, and after that Mother Pearl looked different – a beautiful peace had come over her! This was later confirmed when her three daughters told my husband that, after Shirley's and my visit, they noticed a significant difference in their mom – a soothing calm had come over her and she looked as if she were resting in Jesus's loving arms.

After Mother Pearl's passing, at her request, Shirley Arends and I sang two duets at the funeral service in her Baptist Church. One of the songs was an old hymn called, "In the Garden." Little did I realize then how significant these lyrics would become to me! Following are the words to the hymn:

I come to the garden alone,
While the dew is still on the roses.
And the voice I hear
Falling on my ear
The Son of God discloses.

And He walks with me,
And He talks with me,
And He tells me I am His own.
And the joy we share,
As I tarry there,
None other has ever known.

With the Baptism of the Holy Spirit, I was able to experience those words every day! So, let's continue with how that baptism occurred. It was after the funeral service at a home reception that my life would soon be changed forever.

I was sitting at the kitchen table talking to a man who was a friend of the family. At the time, I was telling him how I had returned to Christianity within the past few years and how joyful I felt that God had shown me in various ways that Jesus was truly His Son. I said there had been an empty void in my life for about twelve years and how fulfilled I felt now that I was again walking with my Lord and Savior. He told me that God had an even greater gift for me, if only I would open my heart to receive it. He said it was called the Baptism of the Holy Spirit!

Then, he explained to me about his experience. He said he had been praying for God to baptize him with His Holy Spirit for a few weeks when a white cloud surrounded him in the shape of his body, and instantly he knew his life would be different from then on. I was so taken by what he said that that night, as I lay in bed, I prayed to God for about two hours that I would be PURE enough and GOOD enough to receive the Baptism of His Holy Spirit. That, I did every night for about two weeks without fail.

And then it HAPPENED! As I lay in bed one night, a white cloud came down over me, in the shape of my body, and I knew God had answered my prayers! I told my husband, who had not had a spiritual baptism, and he said, "Honey, you've been baptized in the Holy Spirit." After that, he had no recollection of what he said. But I will NEVER forget it!

To this day, I've heard of people being baptized with the Holy Spirit, but other than the man in the kitchen, I've never heard of anyone being surrounded by a white cloud in the shape of their bodies. Some have talked about seeing a dove or flames, but never a white cloud. God's Presence in a cloud is mentioned, however, several times in the scriptures.

With reference to the baptism of the Holy Spirit, Jesus tells us in the gospel of John, "Truly, truly, I say to you, unless one is born of Water (water baptism) and the Spirit (baptism of the Holy Spirit) one cannot enter the Kingdom of God." (John 3:5)

It seems there are many views regarding the Baptism of the Holy Spirit. Some churches teach that, when water baptism occurs, one is automatically baptized in the Holy Spirit. But this is not always the case. Others teach that water baptism always occurs BEFORE the Baptism of the Holy Spirit. This also is not always the case. In Acts 10:44-47, we read that the Gentiles received the Baptism of the Holy Spirit BEFORE they were water baptized.

Some churches teach that one is not baptized in the Holy Spirit if they have not received their spiritual language. I know this cannot be true because I didn't receive my spiritual language until a few years AFTER I experienced my Holy Spirit baptism. My spiritual language has never been for prophesy either as some churches believe, but so I can express my thoughts and feelings to God without being hampered by the English language or evil forces.

My point here is not to dispute what others have experienced or believe is TRUTH about the Holy Spirit, but to stress that we should never put God "in a box." He does what He wants, when and how and where and why He wants. Because – REMEMBER – HE IS GOD!!

After my Spiritual Baptism, my life was completely changed! I had an even closer relationship with God than ever before or that I could ever have imagined. He was now living within me, loving me, and guiding my every step. I felt His joy and a peace within me that surpassed all understanding. And I loved my new life!

CHAPTER FIVE

---❤---

Presence of God!

"A cloud overshadowed them, and a voice came out of the cloud.
And God said, 'This is my beloved Son, listen to him.'"
Mark 9:7

A few years after I experienced the Presence of God in a white cloud and received my Baptism of the Holy Spirit, I was appearing at a Christian Women's Club event at a restaurant in Marina Del Rey, California. I was asked to speak and sing two songs – a secular song and, thereafter, a spiritual one. The first selection was my version of the Carpenter's "Top of the World," where I changed the lyrics to: "I'm on the top of the world looking down on creation and the greatest satisfaction I have known is the love that I've found ever since He's been around. My Lord keeps me at the top of the world."

After that, I gave a short Christian testimony, and then I sang a beautiful song written by my friend, Shirley Arends. I changed a few of the words, but mostly the song is Shirley's. The ballad is called, "Complete in Jesus" and the lyrics are as follows:

"Complete in Jesus, how can this be?
What kind of answer is this for me?
My heart is empty, all joy is gone.
Now God this message to me has shown."

Chorus:
The love of Jesus, it will abide.
When others fail me,
He's by my side.
If I will reach out, so Christ I meet,
He gives Himself to me,
And I'm complete."

"If I should feel the need of earthly love
And call out longingly to Christ above.
His Holy Spirit will fill me then,
And though I have no earthly friend – Chorus

"Have you been searching to be complete?
Have you been looking to those you meet?
A hand is outstretched so tenderly.
Will you accept His Love so free? -- Chorus -- And I'm complete in
Him!"

· As I began singing these precious lyrics, something wonderful happened! And I will NEVER forget it! A white cloud AGAIN surrounded me, but instead of appearing in the form of my body, this time the shape was round and circular in nature. The white cloud overshadowed me during the entire presentation, and when the song was over, it disappeared as quickly as it came. The feeling I had throughout was beyond surreal, as I'm sure you can imagine! After that, I asked someone who was in the audience if she had seen the white cloud, and she sweetly responded, "No, but I could see it in your eyes!"

It wasn't until a while after the event, that it dawned on me that this was God's precious and definitive answer to my question, asked so many years before, "IS JESUS TRULY YOUR SON?" My response – Oh, what a Loving Lord we serve! He is always there, answering our every precious prayer! Sometimes in the most spectacular way!

—— ♥ ——

CHAPTER SIX

---- ♥ ----

Mighty Miracles!

"And God did extraordinary miracles"
Acts 19.11

Seeing the Presence of God as a cloud in the shape of my body during my baptism of the Holy Spirit and experiencing God's Presence in the form of a circular white cloud when I sang, "Complete in Jesus," were my most powerful and life-changing miracles! But there would also be many others, some that are almost as astounding. (This is interesting and thought-provoking because in the twelve years I was married to my first husband and having doubts about Jesus, there were none!) Following are other significant miracles that occurred in my life:

One miracle happened, when I was living in Malibu! It was a very hot night, and my home had no air conditioning. Instead of sleeping with my head at the top of the bed, I switched positions to the base, so I could feel the cool ocean breeze on my face. Waking up with eyes closed, and feeling groggy the next morning, I'd forgotten I'd changed positions. So, I turned to what I thought was the middle of the bed, but instead it was the edge. With that, I fell off and onto the floor! On the way down, I hit my temple on the wrought iron pull of my Spanish-style bureau, which was across from my bedside.

The pain I felt in my head was excruciating and I knew, WITHOUT A DOUBT, I was going to die. Tears streaming down my face, I cried out in agony, "Jesus, please help me!" Immediately, I saw a tall, crystal-clear rectangular box come down over me from up above. Suddenly, the pain disappeared, and the tears were gone! And I was instantaneously healed! That was it! I was both astonished and amazed at the same time! I got up praising and thanking Jesus over and over for His holy healing touch. Then I gathered my composure and went about my daily routine, but still astounded by what had happened!

Another time in Malibu, I was praying to God about the scripture, "Perfect love casts out all fear." I asked Him what it really meant because I felt there was a deeper truth associated with those words. I knew deep down I was missing something. Shortly after that, I experienced the most beautiful day I have ever had!

Suddenly, I was completely full of love – love beyond all measure and beyond belief! I was entirely devoid of fear or uneasiness of any kind. My whole being was filled with peace, and joy. And I loved everyone! I felt as if I'd died and gone to Heaven! While this was happening, I went about my day, stopping by to do work for one of my accounting clients. On my way home, I wondered if I would feel this way forever. I sure hoped I would. But, of course, I didn't. The powerful love and pure peace I felt lasted throughout that day and into the next, and then it was gone. It was the most wonderful day I'd ever experienced – so precious and beyond description!

I thank God for that beautiful experience and for letting me know He is forever with me, teaching and guiding me always. I also thank Him for giving me greater insight into the meaning of the scripture, "Perfect love casts out all fear."

At that time and thereafter, He showed me that love and fear cannot dwell together. That, by their very natures, they cannot live side by side. He taught me that, if we have a faint, fragile love, it cannot withstand the onslaught of one of evil's most powerful tools -- FEAR. Whereas, if we have a strong, perfect, peaceful Love, it immediately conquers all fear. This kind of Love comes only from God, and the only way we get it is by having Him more and more in our lives – by knowing him and growing closer to Him! Because GOD IS LOVE!

I find, in my personal life, there is more and more love and less and less fear, the more I trust the Lord. And the more I trust Him, the more He has a chance to show me how trustworthy He really is – which causes my love, peace, and trust to increase even more. It is a beautiful cycle to behold!

I have learned, too, the more I know and trust God, the more I love Him and the more I love Him, the more I have the capacity to love others. And the more I fill my heart with love, the less space there is for fear. This results in fear becoming more and more eradicated from my life. This also is a beautiful cycle to behold!

One time, when I had to have back surgery, I was completely calm as my Jewish friend, Dan, drove me to the hospital. He was amazed at how peaceful I seemed, and he commented about it. What he couldn't comprehend was how completely safe I felt in the loving arms of Jesus, completely devoid of fear. The surgery was far more than successful too because my faith also had an impact on the doctor who performed the operation.

With that said, I still have a way to go to reach what I felt on that special beautiful day given to me by God when He taught me the real meaning of perfect love casting out all fear. This is because there are still times when I become nervous, though I am much calmer than I was in the past. Perhaps I'll have to wait until I get to Heaven. I hope not!

There were other times when I was blessed with God's miraculous healing power. Two of them were when I was living in Athens, Georgia. Once I was cured of an intestinal infection at an Episcopal Church healing service and another time a back injury was healed when I was prayed over at a Bible study meeting in my home. At another Bible study in Florida, I was given the gift to heal someone else, but it happened only once. I could feel God's warmth in my hands as my friend's healing took place. And that was it! I've never experienced that ability again.

The last miracle took place after someone I loved was no longer in my life. His name was Lance and I'd like to share a little about the time we spent together. Lance and I met at a spirit-filled church service in the San Fernando Valley of California. We sat next to each other in the pew raising our hands and praising God, along with the congregation. After the ceremony was over, we talked and later became friends.

Lance shared with me that he had been a drug addict and through prayer with his friends, Paul and Michele, he turned his life around and accepted Jesus Christ as his Savior. He also said he saw a difference in Michele from when he knew her in the past, so he asked her about it. He learned she had been baptized in the Holy Spirit and it had changed her life. Lance said what happened to Michele was so appealing to him that he wanted to have what she had. So, he prayed with her and during their prayer, he received his Spiritual Baptism. During that time, he said he saw the dove of the Holy Spirit.

When I met him, Lance was truly "on fire" for the Lord! He was highly intelligent and lots of fun and we really enjoyed one another's company. It felt good to be with a man with such spiritual depth and understanding and who loved Jesus as I did.

As our friendship grew, Lance began to call me Thumper, after the bunny in "Bambi," and I called him Dobbin. It was a silly, playful thing we did, but it gives some insight into parts of our relationship. I wrote the following lighthearted limerick which describes it: (It's not a true limerick, but it is a humorous verse.)

A LIGHTHEARTED LIMERICK

"There once was a horse named Dobbin,

Who had all the mare's hearts athrobbin.

As he pranced by,

They'd give him the eye,

But nary a glance would he give 'em.

"Now Dobbin was no fickled jumper.

Instead, he was faithful and spoken fer.

He loved not a mare,

But a perky blonde hare,

Who went by the name of Thumper.

"And Thumper really loved Dobbin.

For him only was her heart athrobbin'.

"I wuv you she'd say,

Then tickle and play,

And off they'd go heads abobbin'

"The moral of the story is this:

In commitment there is perfect bliss.

Where oneness is found,

True joy doth abound,

And even a horse and a hare cannot miss!"

"Having fun with Lance as we explored the natural beauty of Yosemite National Park in California!"

Lance and I enjoyed many wonderful times together. We attended a spirit-filled church in Santa Monica, and he led many Bible studies in my Malibu home. He was very gifted in his knowledge of the scriptures. He was also a natural athlete, so we often played tennis, golf, and skied together. This went on for about two years. But then things began to change.

Unfortunately, for some reasons unknown to me, Lance succumbed to the devil's clutches and went back to his drug habit. I never knew which personality I would encounter. It could be the best of times. Or it could be the worst of times. This went on for about a year. With that, I knew we could no longer see each other, and I told him so.

Shortly after that, Lance wrote me the following letter:

Dear Chris,

After we last talked, I sensed we both felt the familiar futility of our past conversations. Chris, I love you, and I don't know if there is any hope for us in the future. There is every possibility you will meet someone else, and I must accept that.

What I haven't done is tell you how deeply sorry I feel for the hurt I've caused you this past year. When I said I saw no villains only victims, it was a premature statement. In this past twelve months, I have clearly been a villain. You are guilty only of your fear, and the manifestation of that in trying to control the circumstances around you. Your virtues so far exceed that one blemish, as to render it insignificant. I'm so sorry that in my smallness I tore you down when I should have been building you up.

As you know, I have never had a relationship with a woman of the richness and quality you possess. Our intelligence was meant to complement one another. Your clear thinking to balance my emotional impulsiveness. And most of all our mutual love of Christ that brought us together.

Please accept my heartfelt sorrow for the pain I've caused you. My prayers are that you will recover and rebound quickly from this tragedy, and that your life will find fresh meaning and purpose. I thank God for the other difficulties in my life right now, for they help keep my mind off that which hurts most.

Will love you always,
Lance

A year later at age forty-two, Lance died due to an overdose of drugs and alcohol. I pray he is with our Lord and has not grieved the Holy Spirit because of his behavior and lost his salvation. What happened was quite disheartening to me and made me feel so very sad -- partly because this was such a waste of a beautiful mind and spirit destroyed by the devil's devious desires and a man's moments of weakness.

The way Lance died shocked me too because I couldn't imagine anyone, after receiving God's Holy Spirit, giving that up. I suppose I was naïve. But it made me realize how much we must protect the gifts God gives us. There are always evil forces out there ready and willing to snatch them away.

What surprised me even more about Lance's death was how it affected me, since he had not been in my life for a while. I found myself weeping for three days straight, and I could not seem to stop. I realized it wasn't healthy to continue like that, so in my despair, I cried out to Jesus, *"Please help me, Lord!"* And this is when the miracle took place!

Instantaneously, I was completely covered in God's Glorious Grace! The tears were gone, and I was completely calm and at peace, as if I had been washed anew! I never wept for Lance again – though I do pray for God's mercy upon him, so he has everlasting life with our Father in Heaven.

Besides God's gracious miracle which healed my grief, another positive element arose out of that! Again, "all things work together for good for those who love the Lord and are called according to His purpose."

My relationship with Lance and its heartbreaking end shook me to the core -- it was a wake-up call that gave me the impetus to take a closer look at MY LIFE. As you've probably detected by now, the choices I made selecting men to share my life were not exactly exemplary or wise. First, a philanderer, then an alcoholic, and then a drug addict.

Not that I was perfect. Far from it! I had my issues, just like anyone else. I could be quite feisty at times and fearful at others, and the men in my life only exacerbated these problems. But, as I've grown closer to God, and allowed Him to lead the way, these weaknesses have been greatly diminished. Today, I am no longer feisty, but I am assertive. I also have very little fear, only because of my trust in the Lord.

But, at that time because things were getting worse, I began to seek out the reasons I was making such poor decisions. It was time to figure it out and then take action to solve the problem.

The first plan of action was to pray and ask God for His help and to PATIENTLY LISTEN and WAIT for His answers. As I did this the Lord, through His Holy Spirit and various other means, began to teach me more about myself and how to proceed.

Eventually, he would lead me to a new career, which would help me become more emotionally mature and make better decisions -- and at the same time enable me to help others do the same. It would also prepare me for the most wonderful part of my life – AND GOD'S GREATEST EARTHLY GIFT TO ME!

— ❤ —

CHAPTER SEVEN

—— ♥ ——

Bounteous Blessings!

"The Lord is a shield for all those who take refuge in Him."
2 Samuel 22:31

There are times we don't realize God's loving and protective hand upon us until we look back at incidents that took place in our past. The following blessings are some that occurred in my life and for which I am ever thankful to our Loving Lord for always being there for me:

1. PROTECTION -- I have always been small and slender in size and still am today. As a child, I was very peaceful, never wanting to hurt or harm anyone. I also was a top student and often helped the teacher with chores. This led to jealousies by other students and left me as prey to bullies who lurked in the shadows.

One day, when I was about nine years old, I was going home from school dressed for a birthday party, when I was attacked from behind by a neighborhood boy. As he began to strike, a sudden powerful strength came over me. I whipped around, dug my fingernails into his cheeks, and flung him to the ground. I then slammed his head against the sidewalk cement several times. When I felt safe, I left and he never bothered me again, though he lived nearby.

My mother when I returned home, rather than being concerned and caring that I was assaulted, was upset because I had gotten my party dress dirty. It didn't seem to bother her at all that I was attacked. This really hurt and made me sad because what I needed was comforting – and what I got was criticism. This happened at various times in my life with her. And yet other times she could be quite loving. It caused me to realize then that I could rely on no one to watch over me. I would have to depend on my own efforts to protect myself -- and the Lord of course who has always been there for me throughout my life, especially when my heart was open to Him. And other times too when I didn't even realize He was there until later.

After that, it happened again! Two girls and one boy, on three separate occasions, tried to beat me up and I was again able to prevail in similar ways, except for the last incident when the girl was experienced in karate. She was high kicking me in the stomach, and I was unable to get to her. But suddenly a big burly bus driver came bounding out of his vehicle. He stopped the girl flat in her tracks and sent her home. "Phew!" I was so relieved someone came to my aid. However, I was quite puzzled when I thought about it later because this was not the bus route, and buses never parked in that area. Was it an angel who helped me? I guess I'll never know, until perhaps when I'm in Heaven. I also later learned when I was in high school that the first boy who attacked me was in prison for raping a girl.

Another time, when I was in Paris, I was at the train station trying to reach my French friend, Jacqueline, from a telephone booth. But she wasn't answering her phone. She was supposed to meet me at the station to take me to her apartment. As I tried to call, French people wanting to use the phone were yelling because I was taking too long. They were really mean and angry! I was close to tears because I was lost as to what to do and I didn't speak French.

Suddenly, a tiny woman appeared and asked if she could help. I think she was French, but she spoke English, so I explained my dilemma to her. She told me she knew where my friend lived, and she'd take me there. To this day, I don't know why I trusted this strange woman. Ordinarily, I would have been quite skeptical. But I remember feeling at complete peace as I accepted her offer to help me. With that, she picked up two of my suitcases, one in in each hand. I felt rather guilty because she was so small, and yet she insisted on carrying my heavy luggage.

I toted only my ski boots, which I hadn't used because there was unusually no snow in Chamonix while I was at Jacqueline's chalet in the French Alps. This turned into a beautiful blessing because I was able to spend most of my time at a Catholic monastery, just up the mountain path from the chalet. Being there was like being in the presence of God! So peaceful.

Back to the little lady. She led me quite a distance to take a bus and then after that to take the subway train. It surprised me because she paid both our fares for the bus and train and insisted on doing it. We then walked down a few streets to the front of Jacqueline's apartment house. She then left me with my belongings and when I turned to thank her for her gracious gesture, she was gone. There was no sign of her! Again, was this an angel? I don't know. But she sure acted like one! And my heart tells me she must have been!

Each time these things happened God's protective arms were around me giving me the help I needed to overcome adversity. And this has happened numerous times over the years. I'm sure glad the Lord was and is by my side blessing me with His supernatural powers and protection! And He always will be, as long as my heart is blameless toward Him!

This reminds me of my two favorite Bible verses: "He who dwells in the shelter of the Most High, who abides in the shadow of the Almighty, will say to the Lord, 'my refuge and my fortress, my God in whom I trust.'" (Psalms 91:1-2) and "He is a shield for all those who take refuge in Him." (2 Samuel 22:31) These verses make me feel safe and secure. They comfort me and bring joy to my heart!

2. SPIRITUAL LANGUAGE – A few years after receiving my Baptism of the Holy Spirit, I was attending a worship service at a Foursquare Gospel Pentecostal church called Church on the Way in Van Nuys, California. I was now often worshipping there but still active in the singles group at Bel Aire Presbyterian church. I also continued to attend Mass at Our Lady of Malibu Catholic Church, as I had by this time for many years. I loved the solemn peacefulness of the Mass, along with the quiet beauty and holiness of its service, and I still do today. But there was something surreal, inspiring, and uplifting at Church on the Way, where hundreds of spirit-filled people, full of love for the Lord, raised their hands in worship to Him!

Though I had been to services at Church on the Way many times before, on this day I received a beautiful blessing from God! The outstanding Biblical scholar, Pastor Jack Hayford, was leading the congregation in praise to our Loving Lord when I was swept up in God's Glory and received my spiritual language. It was beyond wonderful! And I thought, *This Christian life is full of one gift after another! I LOVE travelling this path with God as my guide.*

After the service, I felt as if I were walking four feet off the ground! Today, I speak to God in this way whenever I want to convey my deepest, innermost thoughts, without being hampered by the English language. Receiving one's spiritual language is crucial, too, because it cannot be penetrated by evil forces or intent. Thank you, Lord, for blessing me with this supernatural gift!

3. THEOLOGY CLASS – Another significant blessing occurred when I was taking a theology course at Pepperdine University. Since Pepperdine was a Church of Christ college, they required each student to take two religion classes to qualify for a degree. So, I first took an introductory course to the Bible. Then my second choice was to sign up for an upper-level theology class. I had to get special permission to attend this course, which is what I did. I couldn't figure out why I needed "special permission," but I would soon find out!

On the first day of class, I learned I was the only female and the only undergraduate student in the course. All the others were graduate students, mostly preparing for Christian ministry. Once into it, I realized what a great undertaking this was, with about twenty books of required reading.

After a few classes, I felt completely overwhelmed. I was at home weeping because I felt I was in way over my head. In tears, I considered dropping the course when a word of encouragement told me not to give up. So, I did what I always did at this point in my life -- I cried out to Jesus! *"Lord. Please help me!"* The next thing I knew, I was at the Pepperdine library surrounded by many books, voraciously devouring all the theological nougats these readings offered. There was no longer any fear or doubt I could do whatever was expected of me to succeed in this class!

And soon thereafter the great blessing came! After the mid-term exam, the professor announced to the class that the undergraduate had gotten the highest mark, way above all the graduate students. In the end, I received the highest grade in the course. Wow! That was the best class ever, and Jesus was right there enjoying it with me! And teaching me! What a beautiful learning experience.

4. THE PINK SWEATER INCIDENT -- This is my sweetest blessing of all! It was Good Friday afternoon, and I was shopping for an Easter outfit. I came upon the most perfect pink suit with a matching angora sweater. And I loved it! But unfortunately, the store didn't have the sweater in my size. The salesgirl said they had one at another store and they would send it to me. In those days, they didn't have overnight delivery, especially to northern Malibu, so I accepted that I might not have my perfect Easter outfit after all. Regardless, I still prayed to Jesus that somehow, I would! The next day, a knock came at my front door, and it was a deliveryman with a box containing my pink angora sweater. I KNEW in my spirit, and WITHOUT A DOUBT, it was a simple gift from my sweet Jesus! And in my heart, I could hear Him say, "Here, my child, this is from me." *Thank you, Lord! O, how I love thee!*

5. SWEET LAND OF LIBERTY – One of my greatest blessings is having been born in the United States of America. This country is a true gift from Almighty God to all who live here. To me, it is a shining beacon on a hill spreading the Light and Love of the Lord for all the world to see. We are so blessed to live here, and we must NEVER take for granted the freedoms this nation offers.

This was made abundantly clear to me when I was living in Austria in the late 1980s. I was attending the University of Salzburg studying German and singing with the Dome Cathedral choir. One long weekend, I took a side trip with a tour group to Hungary when it was still behind the Iron Curtain. While there I enjoyed eating Hungarian goulash and meeting the people, especially a Catholic priest from St. Matthew's Coronation Cathedral, for whom I still feel love - to this day!

"Enjoying talking to a kind and humble Hungarian priest from St. Matthew's Coronation Cathedral in Budapest, Hungary."

❤

But looming over the city of Budapest was the crushing blanket of cruel communism. The oppression I felt while there was stifling, overpowering, and suffocating.

All I could think of was men and women should not have to live like this! I was so grieved by the dark cloud that hung over the city, that one night I wept in the Spirit, asking God to free the people in this land where my sweet grandmother, Elizabeth, had been born.

I was so glad when it was time to return to Austria. On our way out of Hungary, we had to pass by many communist soldiers, with rifles in hand. It was terrifying! Once we crossed the border, the other group members must have felt as I did because there were resounding shouts and bursts of applause as we left. There was a deep sigh of relief – we were FREE AT LAST! Thank the Lord, a few years later the Hungarians were freed from the cruel hand of Russian Communism. God forbid that should happen in the United States.

Unknown to many Americans, the communists have been working very hard to do just that -- just as they did when they ruined the beautiful country of Venezuela a few years ago. It is proof of what evil does when it takes over!

Since the early 1900s, evil communist/Marxist forces have been attempting to take over the United States of America. But since 2008 they have had even greater opportunities to strike because there are more communists working within our federal and state governments. Many pretend to be patriotic Americans. In 2020, when they used the Covid 19 crisis to their advantage, they became even more emboldened to wreak havoc. This country has never been closer to a communist takeover than now. And there are too many people who are ignorant of what is going on! The activities in some of our big cities -- burning buildings, lootings, and the defund-the-police movement -- are all being executed with one plan in mind -- to cause chaos and take over this nation. The aim is to make our federal government more powerful by federalizing the police, elections, health care and anything else associated with our lives. The goal is to take power away from the states where we have more control over what takes place. They're doing this so the power hungry can rule with an iron fist from Washington, D.C., just as they do in Moscow and Beijing.

The organizations causing all the chaos are backed by Marxists pretending to care about social justice. They use accusations of racism as one of their weapons to divide Americans to succeed in their evil plot. The idea is to divide and conquer. States like California, Oregon, Washington, Michigan, and New York, have all been victims of the takeover and so far, have been hurt the most.

The open-borders policy is no accident either! It is all part of an attempt by Marxists to destroy a nation that looks to God for guidance. They want control over our thoughts, health care, income, education, etc., and to take away our religious rights, freedom of speech, and the right to bear arms to protect ourselves against a totalitarian government and other evildoers. The Marxists would like to see all of us worshipping the State, rather than our Living Loving God!

If we want the USA to be our "Sweet Land of Liberty," and continue to be a blessing, we must do our part to keep it that way. It is not just the military who are responsible to defend this nation, but it is the responsibility of us all. It is our duty to tell everyone we know what is happening!

It is also our duty to obtain accurate information from honest, reliable sources about what is occurring in this nation and to defend our rights with all our might. There are many news media on the internet and on television who blatantly lie to the American people with misleading headlines and news stories. They, and others, also hide important information to protect their cohorts, while at the same time censoring, suing and imprisoning patriotic Americans, especially Christians and conservatives, who don't agree with their views. Some are treated as if we were living in communist China.

So, I'll say it again because I can't stress it enough – BE SURE TO GET ACCURATE INFORMATION FROM RELIABLE SOURCES! And don't believe most of what you read on the internet. Many bits of information we google are filled with biased information and statistics, so we can't even trust that anymore.

It is our responsibility to stay well-informed, so we elect competent patriots who love our country. It is important to look at what they DO and have done in the past, not what they SAY now, as we cast our ballots for them. It is also our duty to ensure that our elections are honest and uncompromised. And to NEVER allow what happened in the 2020 election to happen again.

Each of us has a responsibility, as citizens of this country and as Christians to protect, with courage and fortitude, this great nation established by the Living Lord Himself. BOTTOM LINE: This is a fight of good vs. evil and it's up to all of us, with God as our Guide, to do our part to destroy the evil. Together, we can do it! And with the Lord's help, we will prevail. Are you with me?

AUTHORS NOTE: A significant amount of prayer, with confirmation from the Holy Spirit, has gone into what I've said in this section. And I have only touched on the subject. Though I have elected not to name names or organizations trying to destroy our nation, there is a multitude of irrefutable evidence available to substantiate what I've written -- which does name names and organizations. And there is far more occurring than what I've mentioned – people's rights are being trampled upon just as is done in Russia and China. Their homes are raided, and some are put in jail on trumped-up charges without due process. And some lives are ruined because to defend themselves they must incur exorbitant legal fees against untrue and frivolous lawsuits. For further information, contact or watch NEWSMAX cable TV or the EWTN Catholic TV channel, which has released two documentary films on the subject. TBN (Trinity Broadcasting Network) programs also at times give information about this very serious situation as well.

To anyone reading this book who is a Christian, I say this: It is your solemn duty to God to do ALL you can to stop the travesty that is taking place in our nation! If all Christians and patriotic citizens unite, there are enough of us to make a difference to stop the evildoers who are trying to destroy our country. This is not a time to be fearful, but a time to fight for the land God has given us. This is not a time to sit back while our nation is stolen out from under us. This is not a time to stick your head in the sand because it's uncomfortable to face the facts. You will be far more uncomfortable if you find yourself living under a dictatorial regime like I experienced in Hungary. This is a time to have courage and show your gratitude to God for giving us this great nation by protecting it in every way. Otherwise, it will no longer be the land of the free and the home of the brave!

6. FAMILY -- Though I have twice lost my nuclear family, God has placed in my path so many dear friends who are like mothers, brothers, and sisters to me. I feel so loved that even when I'm alone, I am never lonely. My greatest love, of course, comes from our Father God, my sweet Jesus, and His mother, Mary. All their love far outweighs any I've lost, as they wrap their arms around me every moment of every day!

Friendship with Jesus is a two-way street. He relies on our giving to and loving Him as much as we rely on His Loving and giving to us. Every good relationship has equal give and take on both sides. I can't stress that enough. Remember that as you share your precious life with others.

"Thank you, Mother Mary, for giving birth to our Messiah!"

Besides Jesus, I pray to our Blessed Mother every day. I thank her for loving us and for being our mother and then I say, "Holy Mary, mother of Jesus, please pray for us and our nation now and always." And she responds, "I will, my child." Sometimes I tell her I love her, and in my heart, I hear her say, "I love you, too."

Our Blessed Mother is here with outstretched arms ready to embrace us with her maternal love. Though some have mothers who have disappointed us, she is always there waiting to help. All we need do is pray to her and she will intercede, if our wishes coincide with the will of the Father. She is truly our mother, and she will never disappoint us!

Since I had the role of the Blessed Virgin Mary in the play, *The People Versus Christ*, I have felt a very special closeness to her. On stage for about an hour, I had many lines throughout and I was Mary before she conceived Jesus until His death on the cross.

Mary went from a lighthearted young innocent happy-go-lucky fourteen-year-old girl to a forty-eight-year-old mother in deep despair over the cruel death of her son. The play ends with her heart-wrenching cry of anguish, "Jesus, my baby boy."

Throughout the drama, I strongly felt the Presence of the Holy Spirit, and it was the best acting I've ever done because it wasn't me, but God living through me, that did it! Throughout the play, I was lifted into another realm – it was beyond surreal. I feel so honored and very blessed to have been chosen to play that part!

With my friends and other loved ones here and in Heaven and my sweet Jesus, Mary, and our Father God, I now have a FAMILY forever – a family that will never leave me nor forsake me!

—— ♥ ——

My Special Angel!

"For He will give His angels charge of you
To guard you in all your ways."
Psalms 91:11

During the time I was going to Bel Aire Presbyterian Church, the singles group had a Saint Valentine's Day performance and in it I sang, "My Special Angel." The heartfelt lyrics were, "You are my special angel sent from up above. The Lord smiled down on me and sent an angel to love." I didn't know it then, but God would one day send me that special angel.

In the meantime, I had written a list of qualities I prayed the man of my dreams would possess. I asked that he be spiritual, kind, gentle, intelligent, have a sense of humor, be financially stable, enjoy classical music, and play tennis and golf, and liked to ski. The qualities went on and on. A male friend who had seen my list, one time jokingly said, "It might be a while before we experience the second coming of Christ." I laughed at what he said, but I also knew, "With God, all things are possible."

About this time, I received a message from someone who wished to remain anonymous. To this day, I don't know how I came upon it, but I loved what it said! I've changed some of the thoughts to make them clearer, but this is the gist of it:

Everyone longs to give themselves completely to someone else – to have a deep soul relationship with another – to be loved thoroughly and exclusively. But God, to a Christian says, "No, not until you are satisfied, fulfilled and content with being loved by me alone – by giving yourself totally and unreservedly to me -- will you be ready to love another. Not until you are first content to be united with me – exclusive of anyone or anything else – will you be ready for someone else. I want you to stop planning and allow Me to give you the most thrilling existence – one that you cannot imagine. I want you to have the best! Please allow me to bring it to you. Just keep watching and expecting great things. Keep experiencing the satisfaction that I Am. Listen to and remember the things I tell you. Just wait! That's all! Don't be anxious. Don't worry. Don't look around at what others have gotten or I've given them. Don't look at the things you THINK you want. Just keep looking up to Me, or you'll miss what I want to show you. And then, when you are ready, I'll surprise you with a love far more wonderful than any you could dream of. You see, until you are ready, and until the one I have for you is ready (I am working even now to have both of you ready at the same time), until you are both satisfied exclusively with Me and the life I have prepared for you, you won't be able to experience the love that exemplifies your relationship with Me, and is, thus the PERFECT LOVE!"

I was quite moved by this message. I took it to heart and decided to heed what it suggested. It certainly sounded like sage advice. And it certainly sounded like something God would say!

Meanwhile, with those ideas in mind, I continued my service for the Lord at the Bel Aire church. I also continued working with my accounting clients, though I was beginning to ponder whether accounting was what God wanted me to do for the rest of my life.

I began to pray seriously about this when the Lord put it upon my heart that, "Yes," it was time for a big change to take place. It was not only a new career He was suggesting, but more of a CALLING! Something that would not only bless me, but also fulfill His purpose for my life in service to Him and to others forever.

I think about this now and realize that, had I not had faith and listened to and trusted God's guidance, I never could have fulfilled my dreams and the Lord's purpose for me and His plan for my future. The more I thought about what the Lord placed upon my heart, the more I realized the decision to make such a drastic change was not really going to be that difficult. I was actually quite excited about the prospect of a new adventure that would allow me to serve our Heavenly Father even more! And I really trusted that God would be there with me every step of the way. That gave me great courage to move forward with His plan.

As I prayerfully moved forward to satisfy God's urgings, in numerous ways the Lord showed me that psychology should be my chosen field of study. So, I signed up for a psych class at Pepperdine while I investigated the possibilities for graduate school. After this, I had an opportunity to attend Harvard University in Cambridge, Massachusetts to study abnormal psychology and statistics, which would count toward my graduate degree. While there, I completely engrossed myself in my studies.

Going to Harvard was particularly significant because one of my prayers about college had been to attend that university. Another prayer was to get my doctorate in Theology from Princeton University in New Jersey. This prayer has not yet been answered, but that's okay. Jesus teaches me every day and that's enough for me!

He's the best professor of all. Especially when it comes to theology! Perhaps someday Princeton will bless me with an honorary degree since I'm being taught by the top teacher in the universe! I may be joking, but it IS true!

Before and after my Harvard experience, I continued to research which university to attend to obtain a graduate degree in mental health. After much prayer, I knew without a doubt through a heart consciousness from the Holy Spirit, that my chosen graduate school would be the University of Georgia in Athens, Georgia. I was really happy about that because, since I lived in Connecticut, for some unknown reason, I'd always wanted to live in Georgia.

With faith believing and without enrolling at the school, I rented out my Malibu home, packed my bags and hopped on a plane to Georgia. I had no doubt this was what the Lord wanted me to do, and I had complete peace about it as I flew across the country to my new destination. Once there, I had no problem getting started, which is the way things go with God leading the way!

Since I had to be accepted into and decide which of UGA's many mental health programs would be right for me, I signed up for two psych courses which would count toward my degree. I wanted to carefully choose the program that would most fit what God intended me to do. Would it be social work, clinical psychology, or counseling? After more prayer and God's guidance, I chose counseling because it would lead to becoming a psychotherapist – a field that would help me in my life and allow me to help others and serve the Lord. I therefore applied to UGA's education department where the specific courses I needed in mental health counseling were available. This was in September at the beginning of the school term.

Within a short time, I found a decent place to live, began my studies, met new friends, and started attending a Baptist church. My life was right on schedule, and I was enjoying my new adventure with God by my side.

On November 8th, it was my fiftieth birthday, and I was at a restaurant celebrating with another graduate student, who was getting her degree in social work. We discussed our career goals and wanting to share our lives with a "significant other" someday.

That night, as I lay in bed thinking about our conversation and praying about meeting that "special someone," the most wonderous happening occurred! A voice from Heaven spoke to me and said, "In five years, you will meet the man I've chosen for you." It was not an audible sound I heard, but more of a heart and mind consciousness. It was, however, definitely God speaking to me! The Divine Voice, incidentally, is not always expressed in words. Many times, it comes through a heart consciousness. Mine though seemed to come through both my heart and mind.

By this time, I was used to God's guidance, so I wasn't shocked to hear His voice. But what I couldn't believe was that I would have to wait until I was fifty-five years old to meet the man of my dreams. I said, "But Lord, I'll be so old by then." I'm sure He chuckled at my response and then ignored me. Now I look back and think that age fifty-five was not really that old. And once you have eternal life, age is rather insignificant.

After that, I began two years of intensive study toward my graduate degree. During this time, I was also chosen to do my internship at UGA, which was an honor since only one person per year was selected. I worked as a mental health counselor with students, and I loved that job! It was extremely rewarding! I thank God to this day for the opportunity to do that!

Once I received my degree, I was ready to get on with my life! But then the next questions were, "What do I do now?" and "Where do I go next?" After much prayer and investigation, I felt led by the Lord to move to a specific town in south Florida. So, I returned to

Malibu for several months, sold my home, and soon after left for the Sunshine State to start my new career as a psychotherapist.

When I arrived in Florida, I rented a condo and got a job as a counselor at a children's psychiatric hospital. This was not a Christian facility, so within a year, I resigned. I strongly felt it was important to combine spiritual and mental health counseling to heal the whole person. Because of this, I decided to go into my own practice as a Christian psychotherapist.

I was able to do this because by that time I was working at St. Paul of the Cross Catholic Church in North Palm Beach where I led group therapy sessions. The meetings were for people who were separated and divorced. As you know, this was right in my wheelhouse since I had plenty of life experience in THAT area! So, it became my specialty. After I left the psychiatric hospital, I was given an office at the church where I saw clients. I also saw others in my home. Though I specialized in separated and divorce therapy, I saw children and married couples, too.

This was an extremely rewarding and fulfilling time for me! I was completely happy serving God through my work. And I was no longer longing for someone to share my life! My God was my ALL – and I was completely content living my life with Him and helping others. I thought of myself as a nun, but with better accommodations! However, I was casually dating at the time, so I guess it doesn't quite qualify me as a nun.

With this in mind, I did occasionally wonder whether God's message to me about His "chosen man" would occur. And I sometimes thought, "Gee, what if it were all my imagination?" Although any other time God had spoken to me in the past, it was always His voice through His Holy Spirit that I heard.

84

Almost five years had passed since I'd received the Lord's promise about His "chosen someone." I had been renting in Florida for over a year by now. So, because of this, I decided it was time to buy a condo. I loved the area where I lived so I chose to buy a home in the building next door to the one where I was renting.

By this time, I was coming upon my fifty-fifth birthday – WHICH THEN CAME AND WENT! So, I thought, "Wow, it WAS my imagination!"

What I didn't realize until later was that someone had called to wish me, "Happy Birthday," on November 8th. By mistake, she called the telephone that was mine at my former rental. She then remembered I had a new phone number and quickly dialed me at my new address. My friend said she talked to a nice man who was now living at the rental, and he told her he had gotten numerous calls for me. She mentioned it might be a good idea to phone him to give him my number, so he could give it to people trying to contact me. She also thought he might be a possible dating prospect. I laughed and said, "He's probably too young, too old, or married." And I brushed it aside.

A few days later though, on November 12, I thought about it and decided it might be a good idea to call my former residence to give the new occupant my phone number in case there were others trying to reach me. I had also been missing a blanket and frying pan since my move, so I wanted to ask him if I'd left them there. When I called, the man to whom I spoke was quite pleasant. I gave him my phone number and he said he would check to see if he could find my lost items and then get back to me.

Soon after, we talked again on the telephone. And we began to have a relaxed and friendly conversation. I learned he was a physicist and engineer who worked at Kodak in Rochester, New York, and he was on special assignment in Florida. He said he was about to take early retirement and planned to stay in Florida once he retired. We discussed many things about our lives and from what he said I surmised he was approximately my age. His voice was gentle, and he seemed to be a kind, intelligent man. He enjoyed skiing and he also liked to play tennis and golf. He also played the guitar and piano and loved classical music. What was surprising was that we both attended the same Catholic Church, where I was a counselor, even though there were other Catholic churches much closer to our homes. He also told me he was separated from his wife who lived in Rochester. Before ending our conversation, we talked about playing tennis together, and he asked if I would like to go out for supper sometime. I said I would like that. After an hour and a half of talking, we hung up!

The conversation was so easy and enjoyable I felt I'd known this man all my life. And to my amazement, my heart was filled with so much love for him I knew I would love him as a friend forever – no matter what! I had never experienced anything like this before. It was astounding and I was completely shocked! I thought, if this is my "special someone" God has chosen for me, "I don't care if he's short, fat and bald. I love him."

When I got off the phone I said to God, "This is really baffling to me! I know this may sound strange and I don't understand it, but I feel so much love for this man. I know this is completely opposite of what I would tell my clients, but I love him and I'm going to love him for the rest of my life!" The love I'd felt was not romantic but deep and spiritual -- like the love I felt on that special day given to me by God – and even like the love described in that anonymous note!

A short time after that, we met, and hallelujah! He was NOT short, fat, or bald (though it wouldn't have made a difference in my feelings for him). He was 6'1" tall with brown hair and beautiful big brown eyes and an adorable face. With all that, I still wasn't sure he was "the one." After all, he was married, and even though he said he was separated from his wife, I didn't think God would send me a married man. Then I thought, *Perhaps God wants me to help him and his wife to get back together. Maybe that's why we've met.* I was willing to do whatever God wanted. And the love I felt for this man was so deep, so pure, so holy, so "from God," that all that mattered to me was to do whatever was best for him.

After that, we played tennis and then we talked for a while. Since he was separated and since I was a counselor specializing in separated and divorce therapy, I offered to help him and his wife with their problems, if it were something he wanted to pursue. But he said they had been to counseling numerous times and she was only interested in "fixing" him, rather than working on her own issues. He also said some things had happened in the past year that made him realize there was no hope for them because he didn't want to be with her anymore. He said the main reason he moved to Florida was to get away from her. And that was why he persuaded Kodak to send him on this special assignment.

After that, we spent a lot of time together and we became close friends. He was the perfect gentlemen. And he had a sweet, easy-going temperament, which was a positive for my personality. We had lots of fun and he had a great sense of humor. We were always laughing and joking, and it was a pleasure to be together! He was such a gentle soul! I probably could have allowed myself to fall in love with him during this time, but I held off because he was still married, and I wanted to get to know him better. Also, because of my past history with men, I wanted to be extremely cautious. I would just prayerfully wait and watch!

So, I watched and waited. A few months later, he was on a business trip to Rochester, but he made it a point to fly back to Florida early, so he could take me out for dinner on Valentine's Day. I was quite surprised to hear from him but also very happy that he wanted to be with me on that special day. I was also glad I didn't have another date.

So, once I was sure he (Thomas Garaway Seckel) had made serious plans to get a divorce, and once I knew he was deeply in love with me, I allowed myself to fall deeply and romantically in love with him on -- Saint Valentine's Day!

Yes, Tommy was truly my special angel sent from up above! God had kept His word that I would meet His chosen man in five years! And to boot -- we were both fifty-five years old, though Tom was two months younger than I. I chalk that up to God's sense of humor because I had suggested in my long list of wishes that I might like someone who was younger than I, rather than some "old fogey." Talk about being picky! The Lord actually fulfilled EVERY desire on that wish list I'd written so many years prior to meeting Tom. And He added things I didn't even know I needed. God is so good!

Years before I met Tommy, my special song was the following, and after he was in my life, it became, "our song:" It perfectly described my feelings at the time!

"When I fall in love, it will be forever

Or I'll never fall in love.

In a restless world like this is,

Love is ended before it's begun.

And too many moonlight kisses

Seem to cool in the warmth of the sun.

When I give my heart

It will be completely,

Or I'll never give my heart.

And the moment I can feel that

You feel that you feel that way too,

Is when I'll fall in love with you."

This song perfectly conveys my heartfelt feelings before I met Tom and continues to this day!

Incidentally, during the five-year wait, the Lord showed me that sometimes we must be patient when we pray for something because He needs time to work out certain details in the best way for us. God also revealed that our lives are so linked up with others that He needs time to work out their situations, too. I know I was not ready to meet Tom until five years later and neither was Tom ready to meet me. It was God's perfect timing! Of course.

What always amazed me too about Tom is, though he didn't have my kind of relationship with the Lord, he always understood and accepted that I often heard God's voice. And when I said the Lord spoke to me, Tom LISTENED! Never questioning, never doubting! He truly BELIEVED, which only confirmed he was my special angel sent from up above!

"JOYOUS OCCASION – Our wedding day!!"
MR. and MRS. THOMAS GARAWAY SECKEL

———— ♥ ————

"After almost three years of heart-warming happiness, Tommy and I were married at a civil ceremony in Palm Beach Gardens, Florida on October 24, 1994. Our desire was to be married at St. Paul of the Cross

Catholic Church in North Palm Beach where we attended, but Tom's annulment hadn't yet come through from the church, so we set aside our desires and settled for a civil ceremony. It took place behind the Palm Beach Gardens courthouse on a lovely large grassy patch, with palm trees blowing in the breeze, on a beautiful, sunny day!! It didn't matter that it wasn't in a church either because it became a holy place for us after all. Jesus and our Father God were right there with us as we prayed and read the Scriptures with our dear friends, Mary and Joe, and the sweet, lovely lady who presided over the ceremony! After that, the four of us celebrated at the beautiful, luxurious Ritz-Carlton Hotel.

"Incidentally, even though our marriage ceremony didn't have the solemn church service we wanted when we married, we did have that joy a year before at our engagement Mass. We experienced then the serene holy beauty that only a Catholic Mass contains, when God blessed us with a lovely communion service at my mom and dad's Catholic Church in Utica, New York. With many family members attending, it was just like a wedding service! The same priest whose prayers had brought about my father's conversion, presided over the ceremony, and it was beyond beautiful! Afterward, we all enjoyed a lovely engagement reception at a local Utica restaurant. (This event occurred a few years before the sad break-up with my mom and sister.) And I thank God for those special memories!!

"I don't remember why it took so long because I certainly prayed about it, but Tom and I finally did have a church wedding ceremony on October 28, 2000, at St. John's Episcopal Church in Franklin, North Carolina, where Tom and I owned our mountain home. Perhaps it was God's will that we wait until we were at that special church that had so much meaning for us then and still has! Afterward, there was a reception with many beloved parishioners, whom we love to this day!"

"AN INTERESTING SIDE NOTE -- When I became MRS. THOMAS SECKEL, I was wondering about the origin of the name, "Seckel," because the name was unfamiliar to me. When I investigated, my findings were quite fascinating, especially when one considers my story! The name, "Seckel," (Sekhel) actually means "wisdom" in Hebrew. Though Tom was brought up as a Christian by his Christian mother, there was Judaism in his background through his father's father. This only shows me that with God, there is so much more depth and meaning in our lives, if we will only seek to find it." JUST ONE MORE AMAZING BIT OF INFORMATION AFTER ANOTHER – "I'm in awe of our Mighty God and how orderly He is as He weaves the patterns of our lives into His Holy perfect whole!!"

— ♥ —

"Enjoying skiing and each other on our honeymoon in Breckenridge, Colorado!"

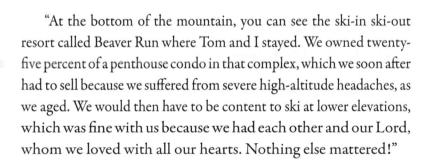

"At the bottom of the mountain, you can see the ski-in ski-out resort called Beaver Run where Tom and I stayed. We owned twenty-five percent of a penthouse condo in that complex, which we soon after had to sell because we suffered from severe high-altitude headaches, as we aged. We would then have to be content to ski at lower elevations, which was fine with us because we had each other and our Lord, whom we loved with all our hearts. Nothing else mattered!"

"It wasn't until February 1995, that Tom and I finally went on our honeymoon to Breckenridge, Colorado. We had a beautiful God-blessed time enjoying the magnificent Rocky Mountains and the lovely little town of Breckenridge.

What a joy those years were as Tommy and I dated, became engaged, and married! The following is a poem I wrote just after he and I were wed:

Dear God,

From whom all good gifts come.

The greatest through Your Loving Son!

Thank You for Your Love, Your grace.

For joy's inviting, radiant face!

For Love in this world –

My Tommy, my ground.

Your warmth and light

In him abound!

Cleanse me now from sin and strife.

Give me grace to lead my life –

In Love, in peace, in strength –

In holiness.

My years together with Tommy were magical! We were never apart because we wanted to make up for all the years we'd missed. A day never went by when we did not hug or tell the other, "I love you," often. We were so grateful to God that we were in each other's lives.

Our first Christmas was my best Christmas ever! And those thereafter came in a close second with Tommy by my side. We had many wonderful adventures together: Skiing, playing tennis and golf and attending musical theater productions.

We moved from South Florida and bought an historic home in Savannah, Georgia, where we lived for three years. It was built in 1888 and had fireplaces in every room, including the kitchen, which I loved! Our home was located next to the square where there is a gazebo, and Tom and I were able to enjoy many weddings that took place there. We could also watch the famous Saint Patrick's Day parade each year, which took place just two blocks away. And the fireworks at the harbor on special holidays were spectacular!!

While in Savannah, we attended Mass at Saint John the Baptist Catholic Cathedral and Tom and I both sang in their choir. This was particularly special to me because I'd always wanted to sing in a choir with my significant other. Tommy also enjoyed being in the choral group. It reminded him of when he sang in his Presbyterian Church all-boys' choir when he was growing up in Buffalo, New York. Tom and I loved living in Savannah where we could walk everywhere, especially to church.

Unfortunately, two years later, criminal activity in Savannah significantly increased because the new mayor was not nearly tough enough on crime, as the previous one had been. And the crime rate went up drastically! After a girl was raped in front of our home and another woman shot in the face and killed a block away, it became terrifying to live there. So, we decided to look for safer surroundings.

"So happy together at our historic Savannah home!"

"(Incidentally, I never did find out what happened to my blanket or my frying pan, but I did find a new friend forever! And I praise God for that every day!!)"

—— ♥ ——

"Gazebo near our residence at one of Savannah's many beautiful public squares!"

I learned from this experience why it is so essential to take seriously those we vote into office.

After that, we moved to Athens, Georgia for a while until we designed and built a beautiful home in the Franklin, North Carolina Nantahala Mountains, where it was a joy to live! However, the winters were too cold for Tom, so we later also built and designed another home on a forty-seven-acre tree farm in Live Oak, Florida, where we spent the winter months. We worked many hours on the land and decorating our dwellings, and we enjoyed every minute of it – because we were together!

We also were thankful to meet some very special people in those two areas. It was especially fruitful because we were able to share our story with them about the Lord we love so much and how He impacted our lives. The more people we met, the better it was because we had more opportunity to tell them how much God loves us all.

Wherever we went, we never forgot our commitment to God. He was always with us -- even when we were enjoying earthly adventures! Our life was filled with prayers of thanksgiving to God for bringing us together and for all His blessings. We spent many hours praying for others, attending church, studying the Scriptures, and going to Bible studies.

And though we were basically Catholic, we worshipped at other churches, too, because we realized the body of Christ comes from many different Christian denominations. These churches are filled with people who love the Lord with all their heart, soul, mind, body, and spirit. And, though there are some in ALL denominations who are Christians-in-name only – who attend church but have no real relationship with our Loving Lord – these churches are filled with many members who DO have a thriving relationship with Christ. Though God wants us to attend a church that abides by His Word and commandments, what is of ultimate importance to Him is what we feel in our hearts. Are we loyal to Him and do we love Him with all our heart, soul, mind, body, and spirit? And do we love our neighbor as we love ourselves?

We realized, too, that though we can often guess through another's actions the kind of person they are, it is not up to us to judge someone else's heart. The heart of man is so delicate and complex that only its Maker can truly know it. It is God who will judge us all one day. He alone will look at whether our hearts are filled with love, first and foremost for Him and His Son and then for others -- or for the unholy things of this world. So, we left that part for our loving Lord to decide!

I learned that we must come to God with a child-like attitude. That we must be child-like (and not childish) in our treatment of others – full of joy and laughter, and devoid of criticism. Jesus said after calling to a child and putting him in the midst of them, "Truly, I say to you, unless you turn and become like children, you will never enter the kingdom of heaven. Whoever humbles himself like this child, he is the greatest in the kingdom of heaven." (Matthew 18:3) Therefore, we are to be humble, friendly, and loving to all – not critical or fearful.

That's not to say we become naïve either. Jesus also said, "Behold, I send you out as sheep in the midst of wolves; so be wise as serpents and innocent as doves." (Matthew 10:16, KJV) We must always be cautious and wary of danger, yet loving, as we wend our way through life spreading the joy of the Lord to all we meet.

Along with the Catholic Church, we visited Baptist, Episcopal, Assemblies of God, and many other churches, where Tom and I enjoyed Bible studies and potluck dinners with kind, loving people.

One of those we attended was St. John's Episcopal Church in Franklin, North Carolina, where Tom and I went whenever we were at our mountain home. This tiny church is a shining example of Jesus's teachings as it opens its loving arms to all who pass through its portals. We treasure many memories spent with its members. And we will be there again someday because its cemetery will be Tom's and my final resting place here on Earth.

Though our lives were about as happy as any could imagine, that doesn't mean everything was always perfect. It was not. Life here on Earth is NEVER perfect. Tommy and I had our weaknesses, as do we all. But the issues we had were minor compared to the great love we shared. And we had peace within those difficulties because we trusted our Lord to handle them. Mostly though, our life was beautiful because it was blessed by God.

What was also important for Tom and me to realize was that our love and loyalty to each other should never be greater than our love and loyalty to our Father God and our Lord, Jesus Christ. He and I had a conversation about this, and I explained to him what I knew and felt. I was also aware that my deep love for Tom was only possible because I first loved my Lord and my God, above and beyond anything else.

As the years went by and we grew older, Tommy and I realized it was time to downsize and enjoy a simpler lifestyle. So, we decided to sell our two homes and move to a condominium. In doing so, we chose to go back to south Florida where we had had so many wonderful memories. We first looked for a rental before we bought one. And fortuitously we ended up at the same condominium complex where our romance began! It was the same building where I had rented, and Tom had rented after me. Can you believe it? And the apartment next door to our rental was for sale. It was exactly what we wanted, so we bought that! It couldn't have been more perfect. Because we prayed with faith believing about everything, it had to be God who made all this happen! Here we were back where we began -- twenty-one years before. We had come full circle! Amazing!

Some people wait a lifetime for the love and life Tommy and I had together. And I treasure and thank God for all the moments we shared. Those were the happiest years of my life! But sadly, one and a half months after moving into our new home, we received bad news. Tommy was very sick. He went into the hospital on Saint Valentine's Day, twenty-one years to the day since I fell in love with him. And he would live for only two more months. On April 22nd, my sweet angel left this life to live with our Lord forever.

The pain of that was indescribable, but my Lord Jesus and my friends Cyndi, Mary, and Mary Ann got me through it. And Tom's daughter, Tamara, who is now my daughter and a special gift Tommy left me, has been there for me, too. Her love, thoughtfulness and support far outweigh any love lost from the past by my daughters! I pray for her and her husband, Jon, every day, along with Tom's son, Tim and his wife, Andrea, and Tommy's grandchildren, Avery and Livy.

It was also a Bible study I attended that helped me tremendously as I plowed through those days. It became the highlight of my week during that difficult time. Judy Schalk, whom God gave the precious gift of teaching, was the Bible study leader, and she did an outstanding job! Her friendship was a godsend to me. Judy is now in the northeast sharing her talents at Coastal Christian Church, in Ocean City, New Jersey, which is a congregation "on fire" for the Lord.

At that time, I couldn't go to Mass because I would weep through the whole service. Instead, I watched it on the Catholic station, EWTN (Eternal World Television network), which was also a godsend. I listened to its founder, Mother Angelica, and my favorite priests, Father Joseph Mary Wolfe and Father Mark, whose hearts are filled with Jesus's love.

Christine,
I loved you then,
I love you still,
I always have,
I always will.
Thomas

"This photo was taken of Tom and me when we were visiting friends in Bonita Springs, Florida – just before our lives would be changed forever. (The message with it will be explained later.)"

ETERNAL LOVE NEVER DIES! – "In our older years, when we were in our seventies, Tommy and I visited our dear friends, Wayne and Kimiko, who had moved from upstate New York to Bonita Springs, Florida. It was not long after our fun time with them that my Tommy left our life together to live with our Lord in Heaven forever.

Just after Tom's passing, on one of my more difficult and distressing days, I was filled with sadness because I was questioning Tom's love for me. I needed to feel his loving presence, but I wasn't sensing it at all. It was at this time that I received the message shown with the picture of Tom and me on the previous page. (It would be the last time that he and I would be photographed together.)

"The words, "I loved you then, I love you still," next to the photo were written on a pendant in a brochure that was mailed to Tom just after his passing. It was from a jewelry store, where Tom had had previous dealings. The pamphlet suggested that Tom buy the necklace for me. And those words, "I loved you then, I love you still, I always have, I always will" arrived just when I needed to receive them most. Was it a coincidence? I don't know. But I do know the impact it had on me! And I do know that God is many times involved in what we might call, "coincidences." Some people call them God winks! And they often occur when our hurting hearts cry out for help from God!!

"Afterward, when I thought about it and prayed about it, I concluded what my heart already knew. I KNEW it was the Lord's way of reassuring me of Tommy's unending love. And it was, absolutely, by the GRACE OF GOD, that those words were sent to me at that CRITICAL TIME. The meaningful message has greatly impacted me since then! And from that time on, I have felt my special angel's presence with me every moment of every day! I know I am wrapped in his loving arms FOREVER -- along with the ever-loving arms of GOD!!"

"Since Tommy's passing, I now also listen to TBN (Trinity Broadcasting Network), which has been invaluable to me! The Mike Huckabee Show, Matt and Laurie Crouch, Joyce Meyer, Pastors Robert Morris and Allen Jackson, Joel Osteen, and Dr. David Jeremiah, all teach or confirm to me truth about our Loving Lord through their programs. They are each a blessing from God!

There are many levels of heartbreak in our lives, but there is nothing like the loss of a spouse who was both a friend and soulmate – who was missed the minute he walked out of the room! That heartache is so deep and painful, words can't describe it.

And yet God's healing power takes over and soothes our broken aching hearts. With complete trust in Him, He replaces that pain with His healing Love and the love and caring of others. Through weakness, we are made stronger, and our characters are built so we can serve God even better than before.

I know I am a much better person after the death of my husband. It changed me like no other event could have. And that which did not kill me DID make me stronger. But it was tough – I will not lie!

When something as catastrophic as that occurs, one realizes more than ever before what is truly important. Silly little things no longer matter. It is only the major basics that are crucial, especially one's walk with God and how to improve upon that. Then everything else falls into place.

Had this event not occurred I could not have done the work for the Lord that was expected of me. I was so devoted to my husband I could not have done what God intended because I could not do both. Some people could – I could not. And we are here, basically, to serve the Lord and fulfill His purpose for mankind and that MUST come first.

Through that crisis, I have grown in many ways – in patience and kindness and all the fruits of the Holy Spirit. I feel closer to Jesus than ever before and to His mother, Mary, and to our Father God. My angel, Tommy, is now in Heaven with them. But I feel his presence with me every day. And our hearts still beat as one as we walk together!

With Tommy's passing, I feel as if I have one foot in Heaven and one here on Earth. That's because my greatest loves are up above, and my work on this planet is not done. And when it is, I'll again be with "MY SPECIAL ANGEL!"

—— ♥ ——

Chapter Nine

— ♥ —

Nine Paths to Happiness, Peace, and Joy!

*"Thou dost keep him in perfect peace
whose mind is stayed on thee,
because he trusts in thee."*
Isaiah 26:3

*"Cast all your anxieties on Him
For He cares about you."*
1 Peter 5:7

"In God's Presence is fulness of joy!"
Psalms 16:11

My prayer is that the following nine paths will help in your journey toward a happy satisfying life filled with peace and joy! May God bless you in your endeavors!

1. PRAISE – The first path toward happiness is to begin your day praising and thanking God for all His bounteous blessings! God loves it when we glorify Him and when we do, He inhabits the praises of His people. So, He is right there with you as you lift your heart to Him! It is also a spiritual law that we begin all prayer with praise and thanksgiving to the Lord.

Just as the walls of Jericho fell with the faithful shouts of God's people, your walls of difficulty can also fall away with your faithful praises to the Lord. Fear, depression, despair, and feelings of failure can all be driven out with praise and thanksgiving. Powerful protection is also available when you honor God in this way. So, it is vital if you are to be happy and fulfill God's purpose for you, that you start your day in this way!

My daily routine is always better when I begin it with praise and thankfulness to the Lord. I start with, "Praise You Jesus, praise You Father. Thank You, Jesus, thank You, Father." And go on from there with the rest of my prayers. I also end my day in the same way and at times throughout the hours when needed -- or if I just want to enjoy the peaceful PRESENCE of Almighty God! Which is often!

The highlight of my day is when I lift my arms to the Lord and pray, "Make a joyful noise to God all the earth. Sing the glory of His name! Give to Him glorious praise!" (Psalms 66:1-2)

Did you know that at the sound of Jesus's name all evil flees? This also contributes to a more peaceful existence. So, keep on praising our Heavenly Father throughout the day in the name of our blessed Lord Jesus! This, along with the following paths, are vital as you strive toward a happier life of peace and joy!

———♥———

2. PURPOSE – The next path toward a happy life is to understand and BELIEVE that God made you – and YOU only – for a specific purpose. Having a purpose brings meaning to life and is one factor that leads to happiness.

It is also important NOT to believe the myth that you can BE anything or DO anything you want. This only leads to disappointment. I love football and I sometimes live vicariously pretending I'm a wide receiver or tight end on a football team, but as a 5'2", 114 lb. female, I don't think I'd make the squad. We can't all be professional football players or medical doctors – but we can be and do whatever God uniquely made each of us to be and do!

It is our job to pray and figure out our abilities and do all we can to excel in those areas. This will bring a feeling of satisfaction and result in happiness because it's why God made us in the first place.

Even if there are times when you are not able to go beyond one room because of age or illness, you can still say, "God bless you" to all with whom you speak. This includes phone calls from telemarketers. Doing this gives you a purpose and satisfies your service to God -- which is the greatest accomplishment of all – because it makes others aware God is watching over them. There is great power in prayer, so your pleas for others, even if you are confined to one room, can cause changes throughout the world, and at the same time fulfill one of your greatest purposes for being here. All it takes is your full faith and willingness to do whatever the Lord asks you to do --- along with God's power -- to alter this planet. Our faith and His power go hand in hand and are the only essentials necessary to make a difference in this world.

That is what I did when I was laid up for months with back problems. And I've done it other times, too. There were business calls to people around the world -- in India, Guatemala, Honduras, Mexico, Columbia, the Philippians, and across the USA. One time, I spent an hour and a half talking to a young man in Mumbai, India. He was stuck in his financial office building because there had been a terrorist attack and he couldn't go home. We spoke about many things, but mostly we talked about God. It gives a great sense of satisfaction when we reach out an arm of love to someone else, no matter what our circumstances might be.

So, get to work discovering your unique areas of expertise and ask your friends for their input, too. But mostly pray about it and wait for God's guidance. It is also vital to ask Him to open doors to success, so you can reach your full potential and purpose. REMEMBER – You are unique and unrepeatable! So, make the most of it!

———— ♥ ————

3. POSITIVITY – Strive always to think positively. Try not to dwell on your mistakes or the mistakes of others. Use them only as learning experiences and start over with God as your guide. Try to bury upsetting memories from your past. And do away with thoughts of failure, unkindness, and bitterness. If others have hurt you, push it aside and get on with your life. And don't allow them to take up any more of your precious time. Give everything to God and then leave it with Him.

If you are still telling friends over and over about someone who hurt you, you have not truly given it to God. And you risk alienating others by constantly referring to negative incidents from your past. So, refrain from negativity and try to limit or exclude those people in your life who bring you "down" or have a negative influence on you.

Our Lord tells us to be thankful for ALL in our lives, even the difficulties because those often help us grow in character. Many complain about their husbands, wives, jobs, etc. And the Lord is saying, "Stop griping and be grateful." Many people would be happy to have your job or to have a mate. Your greatest task is to be calm in God's Presence. And to thank our Heavenly Father for your blessings.

Negative thinking and speaking are self-destructive habits that can be eliminated by constantly ruling them out and replacing them with positive ones. Teach yourself to dwell on all the blessings in your life no matter how small and go through the day thanking God for them. Make this a habit! Seek out others who have a healthy outlook on life and surround yourself with those kinds of people.

Remember, as often as possible, to think on things which are pure and sweet and lovely. You do have a choice! So, purposefully refuse to allow all negativity from entering your thought processes and do it all in the blessed name of our Lord Jesus. Evil forces often use negative thoughts and actions to gain control of us, so be vigilant in your efforts to thwart them.

If you concentrate on eliminating the negative and accentuating the positive, your life will be so much better! At first, it may seem difficult to acquire this new habit, but with practice eventually it will become a natural occurrence and something you enjoy doing! It's a challenge. So, take it on with a brave heart!

———♥———

4. PEACEFULNESS – As you go through each day, try to nurture a spirit of peace by trusting God more and more.

If you find yourself worrying and fretting about a situation and there is nothing more you can do to rectify it, give it to God and then let it go. If you again find yourself fussing and fretting about it, that indicates you have not truly given it to God. It also shows a lack of trust in God's ability to handle EVERY situation. So, pray for your faith and trust in God to increase.

All we need is our complete faith in God, along with His power, and mountains of difficulty can disappear, if it's in God's will for it to happen. My motto is "Give it to God and Go Away!" That means leave it with Him and go on your merry way without a care in the world. And NOT taking it back a few minutes or hours or days later.

This is a habit that can be accomplished through practice and prayer. It is helpful, too, whenever you are burdened by your problems, to start praising our Father God and Jesus and thanking them for all your blessings, and don't stop until you feel at ease.

Are you aware that ninety percent of the things about which we worry NEVER HAPPEN? Think about it! Of all the areas about which you fussed and fretted, how many actually occurred?

Not only is worry and stress bad for your physical well-being, but it robs you of peace, happiness, and joy. So, make it your goal to live in as many stress-free moments as you can – PEACEFUL LIVING IS A HABIT WELL-WORTH NURTURING!

——— ♥ ———

5. FORGIVENESS – We, as humans, are usually not completely capable of forgiveness without the grace of God. But, with the Lord's help, it is possible. It's necessary, if you are going

to lead a happy, fulfilling life that you are not hampered by the burden of unforgiveness.

It's important, too, that you do not dwell on the hurt you feel when others treat you with disrespect or abuse you in other ways. When this happens, it's crucial you immediately pray about it and give it to God. And then let it go! And stop talking about it to everyone you meet. If you are still bringing it up, that means you haven't truly given it to God. And you don't trust Him to deal with it. He can handle the situation far better than you. So, strive for forgiveness in your heart and then let it be! Even if the person who has harmed you is not worthy of forgiveness, you deserve the healing and freedom forgiveness brings with it!

We have better things to do with our short time on Earth than to waste it on thoughts of unforgiveness. So, refuse to allow those ideas to enter your mind. Block them out, in Jesus's name! You DO have a choice! And instead, use that time to think about how you can best serve God and others. Fill your mind with thoughts of how you can best work toward your PATH that leads to peace, joy, and happiness. DON'T ALLOW UNFORGIVENESS TO STEAL THAT FROM YOU!

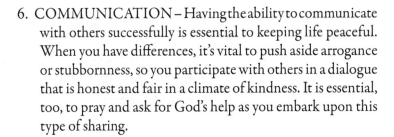

6. COMMUNICATION – Having the ability to communicate with others successfully is essential to keeping life peaceful. When you have differences, it's vital to push aside arrogance or stubbornness, so you participate with others in a dialogue that is honest and fair in a climate of kindness. It is essential, too, to pray and ask for God's help as you embark upon this type of sharing.

Angry outbursts are never an answer to anything when dealing with others. Besides being unchristian-like and immature, it accomplishes nothing. Aggressiveness is never acceptable either in successful communication. And attacking and name calling is an absolute no-no. Rather, successful communication requires that we make our positions known by assertively explaining what we feel in a calm, kind manner and then listening openly to someone else's views. Aggressiveness does not make life easier for anyone. It defeats our purpose to resolve differences and live in peace. But assertiveness can make a positive difference. To be aggressive is to lash out and attack someone without consideration of what they think or feel. It accomplishes nothing, but assertiveness can have the opposite effect.

I've experienced it numerous times, and it is amazing how beautifully assertiveness can bring people closer together. Whereas aggressiveness often shuts down all doors. My incident with the Lutheran pastor in chapter three is a good example of this. When he acted aggressively without full knowledge of the situation, I could have spoken to him later and calmly and assertively talked to him about his disrespectful behavior and explained the facts of the incident, rather than weeping and discussing it with my roommate. Unfortunately, I was too uninformed at that time to know how to handle it.

It's important, too, to understand that the one hundred gracious things we've done for someone are quickly forgotten with one insensitive remark. This could close communication with another forever. So, remember to be kind as you express your feelings and opinions.

Successful communication is a two-way street and if the other person is unwilling to be open and fair, or incapable of rationality, then it's time to stop trying. Sometimes, it's better to sever certain relationships to maintain your own happiness and peace – and to love these people from afar. So, give them to God and go away. Then make it your goal to find others with whom you can more easily share and who have a positive influence on your life.

———— ♥ ————

7. SELF-EXAMINATION – Part of the pathway to peaceful purposeful living is to look at yourself as objectively as possible, so you can become God's version of why He created you.

One way to begin is to examine your life and how you behave or appear to others. Are you talking about yourself and your hurts and needs more often than listening to the needs of others? Do you edify and uplift others? In your actions, are your motivations based on jealousy, selfishness, or revenge? I can't stress enough how vital it is to double and triple check your motivations with ALL actions to be sure they are pure and unselfish.

Also, are you patient and understanding in your dealings with others? Do you become angry over silly things that are meaningless when you look at the big picture? Do you lash out at others because you don't agree with their political or religious beliefs, rather than sitting down and discussing different views? As you communicate, are you closed-minded to other's beliefs and open only to talking about what you THINK is truth? Listening to information from others can be advantageous because you may learn something! But that can only happen if your heart is open to someone else's opinion.

With respect to finances, are you prudent and a good steward with the money and other gifts God has given you? He has not placed these in your hands to be squandered or used irresponsibly. So, carefully examine how you can best use your talents or funds given to you by God. Also, worrying about finances does not help toward your goal of achieving peace and joy. So, spend wisely. And ask the Lord to help you become a better steward of all aspects of the life with which He has blessed you.

Remember, we are the Lord's representatives here on Earth! So, it is our responsibility to nurture the fruits of the Holy Spirit which are love, joy, peace, patience, kindness, goodness, faithfulness, gentleness, and self-control. (Galatians 5:22-23)

This is not easy, but it can be done with God's gracious help! All you need do is ASK HIM! And then try to look at yourself as objectively as possible. See if there are areas upon which you can improve and if you are exemplifying the fruits of the Holy Spirit as you strive to become your very best for God, yourself, and others.

This doesn't mean you will be perfect. Nobody, except God, is perfect. But it does mean your intentions are pure and you are striving to do your very best toward becoming that perfect you, for which you were created by God.

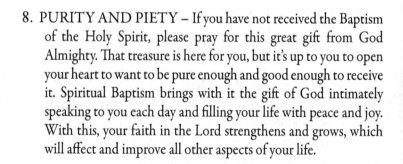

8. PURITY AND PIETY – If you have not received the Baptism of the Holy Spirit, please pray for this great gift from God Almighty. That treasure is here for you, but it's up to you to open your heart to want to be pure enough and good enough to receive it. Spiritual Baptism brings with it the gift of God intimately speaking to you each day and filling your life with peace and joy. With this, your faith in the Lord strengthens and grows, which will affect and improve all other aspects of your life.

With spiritual baptism, your heart softens and changes to where you become completely devoted to God, wanting to please Him in every way and to become holier with each passing day. It brings with it the joy of reading His Word in His Holy Bible and longing to do so. Through it, our Lord's Spirit lives within you and teaches and guides you throughout the day, so you can reach your full potential. This brings with it not only happiness and satisfaction but is also pleasing to God.

———❤———

9. PERFECTLY YOU! – As I mentioned in a previous section, what I mean by being perfectly you, doesn't mean you will reach one hundred percent perfection. We all have our weaknesses, but we can make it our aim to work toward a goal of becoming the person God intended us to be and fulfilling His purpose for our life here on Earth. Work on becoming the best you can be by praying for God's help. The Lord wants more than anything for you to reach your full potential, which brings with it, happiness, satisfaction, accomplishment, and fulness of joy.

You are God's temple! Therefore, you have an obligation to take care of that temple with tender loving care. That means eliminating ALL self-destructive behavior and activities, such as over-eating, smoking, alcoholism, and ingesting drugs, which are obviously self-destructive. Did you know that, because these things are addictive and controlling you, they become your gods -- rather than our Lord overseeing your life and leading you to become the best you can be? Self-destructive behavior and activities also include worry, unforgiveness, stubbornness or anything else that causes stress and takes its toll on our bodies. They are all tools used by evil to gain control over us and ruin our lives.

Other areas important to maintaining a healthy body are exercise and practicing proper nutritional habits, including taking food supplements. Foods you eat can't always give you the nutrients you need, so I suggest taking at least a multi-vitamin, vitamin C and zinc and any others you deem necessary to stay healthy. But when you do, be sure you check with your doctor because some supplements may interact with medications you are taking.

Exercise, not only keeps you at a healthy weight with strong bones and muscles, but it also causes your body to release endorphins, which I call the "happiness pill." As well as giving you a sense of well-being, endorphins also help ward off depression, so you can continue on your path toward happiness.

It's also not necessary to go to the gym or buy expensive exercise equipment or spend extra time exercising. I run around my apartment on my carpet in my bare feet while I'm making my bed and doing other chores around my home. I also do ballet exercises. On my way to the kitchen to prepare a meal, I often do isometric and stretching exercises. In fact, I do this throughout the day. It's important and healthful to keep your blood moving and your heart, bones, and muscles strong so you are in good shape to fulfill your God-given purpose!

Pray for and nurture a habit of walking with God as many moments as possible and pray He will help you develop the positive habits suggested in this book. At first, it may seem difficult, but as you practice, with God's help, soon it will become second nature – just an everyday natural occurrence. Before you know it, you will learn to love and enjoy it!

Each of the paths previously mentioned in this chapter will take practice. So much of our spiritual, emotional, mental, and physical wellbeing depends upon developing healthy and holy habits: Habits that will lead to happiness and to becoming that PERFECT YOU – for yourself and FOR GOD! This will lead to a place where God may smile at you one day and say: "Well done my good and faithful servant. Enter now into the joy of the Lord!" So, get started! There's no time like the present to begin your path toward becoming PERFECTLY YOU!

— ❤ —

Chapter Ten

Labor of Love

"May the Lord bless you and keep you.
May the Lord cause His face to shine upon you,
And give you peace."
Numbers 6:24-26

The years married to my husband, Tommy, were the happiest of my life! But writing this book has been my greatest joy ever! It's been a labor of love to all who peruse these pages. It is my love letter to you, to God, and to ALL the world!

The joy comes from knowing I'm doing what God has impressed upon my heart TO DO! It has brought me a sense of purpose, satisfaction, and fulfillment like no other in my life because I'm telling HIS story – a story about God's bounteous blessings and His magnanimous Love for us all – Love beyond all measure!

This all came about one day when I needed more to occupy my mind after Tommy's passing. I wanted to do something more than cryptic crossword puzzles. And it was no longer enough to say, "May God bless and protect you," to everyone with whom I made contact. It also was no longer enough to share my Christian testimony with the few others who now crossed my path as I plowed through

121

the pages of my life. Though these things were certainly very important! Somehow, I knew it was time to expand my life's purpose if the Lord wanted me to extend my existence here on Earth.

So, one day I boldly blurted OUT LOUD to God, "I need a job!" I told Him I wanted to do MORE for Him. It was just after this that I saw an advertisement on TBN television about their Christian publishing company called Trilogy. The ad was urging people to share their life stories with others.

I had been praying about writing a book for several years to reveal how God had blessed my life in a unique and special way. And I had also been investigating and praying about an appropriate Christian publisher for many months, but until then I hadn't felt comfortable in my spirit with what I'd found. I knew in my heart it wasn't yet the Lord's answer or choice for me.

Once I saw the Trilogy ad, suddenly the words for a publication came pouring into my head. I knew, WITHOUT A DOUBT, it was something God wanted me to do! So, I reached out to Trilogy, and they liked what I proposed.

After much prayer and confirmation by the Holy Spirit, I knew Trilogy Publishing Company was the Lord's choice for me! So, I contacted them again and thereafter signed a mutual contract. I was more than excited about the prospect of working with Trilogy and becoming a part of the TBN family!

I hadn't felt this excited about anything in years! And I was thrilled about this new challenge in my life! It was another God-guided adventure, and the realization that life with the Lord is never boring!

I then started writing and revising and clarifying and editing! And then doing it all over again. It had to be perfect because I was representing God and acting as a channel for Him to speak through me about what He had done in my life. What I revealed had to be His Words, not mine!

I asked Jesus and Mary to partner with me as I wrote it. So, you can talk to them if you have any complaints. Just kidding! But I did ask Jesus and Mary to write it with me and give me their input. That's what having a personal relationship with them is all about!

I also realized, soon after starting, this was an answer to a prayer I'd been saying for many, many years. It's the prayer of Jabez (1 Chronicles 4:10) asking God to bless me and enlarge my borders, so I could reach others for Him. "In the book of Chronicles, verses 9 and 10, it states that Jabez was more honorable than his brothers, so when he called on the God of Israel, praying, "Oh, that thou wouldst bless me and enlarge my border, and that thy hand might be with me, and that thou wouldst keep me from harm so that it might not hurt me," God granted what he asked. I have heard that this prayer, when said daily, is supposed to bring great blessings upon those who pray it. I know it has been true for me! That is why I say it every day and found it especially essential as I proceeded with the pages of this publication.

What was amazing, too, is that as I began this endeavor, I had renewed energy and enthusiasm for life I hadn't had for years. I felt as if I were forty years old again! And that I was performing my greatest purpose for God -- far beyond anything I'd ever done before. Through this book, I saw how everything in my life finally made sense and how God was working and weaving His plan throughout it.

With that being said, the bottom line is this: Your greatest peace and joy come when you allow God to guide you through each moment of every day. And I pray the paths outlined in chapter nine and the suggestions made elsewhere in these writings will help as you strive to walk with Him. As God guides you, these have the potential to help you find true purpose and meaning in your life -- and bring you a sense of satisfaction and accomplishment way beyond your wildest dreams! They can help create complete happiness! And a slice of what it must be like in Heaven!

The Lord has woven the patterns of my life into His perfect whole! So, are you now ready to allow Him to weave yours? Will you spread your wings, going on your merry way – laughing and loving and praying for ALL? Will you be a smiling face for ALL the world to see? And become ALL that God would have you be! AMEN..

In Jesus's most precious Love,

Christine Elizabeth Seckel

—— ♥ ——

"Jesus, I trust in thee!"

Jesus said, "Peace I leave with you.
My peace I give to you."

Gospel of John 14:27

—— ♥ ——

GOD-INSPIRED GOALS

To Reach a Life of Purpose, Peace, and Joy!

— ♥ —

_____

_____

_____

_____

_____

_____

_____

_____

_____

_____

_____

GOD-INSPIRED GOALS

To Reach a Life of Purpose, Peace, and Joy!

— ♥ —

_____

_____

_____

_____

_____

_____

_____

_____

_____

_____

In God's Love,

Christine Seckel

CPSIA information can be obtained
at www.ICGtesting.com
Printed in the USA
LVHW051542070722
722844LV00010B/743

9 781685 565770